1999
Anglican Book Centre
600 Jarvis Street
Toronto, Ontario
M4Y 2J6

Copyright © Anglican Book Centre

All rights reserved. No part of this book may be reproduced, stored in a retrieval system, or transmitted, in any form or by any means, electronic, mechanical, photocopying, recording, or otherwise, without the *written permission* of the publisher.

The layout for "Let Us Give Thanks" was prepared by Best Business Solutions.

TABLE OF CONTENTS

Introduction i

Preparation for the Liturgy 1

The Gathering of the Community 5

Proclamation of the Word 15

Prayers of the People 23

Confession & Absolution 27

The Peace 29

The Preparation of the Gifts 31

The Great Thanksgiving 37

The Communion 51

The Concluding Rite 55

Appendix 1: Liturgical Colour 59

Appendix 2: Incense 61

Appendix 3: Bread Recipes 65

Appendix 4: Resources for Singing the
Gradual Psalms 67

INTRODUCTION

Since the earliest days of the Church, the celebration of the Sunday Eucharist has been the weekly constituitive act of the whole People of God. The gathering of local Christian communities on the Lord's Day for the Lord's Supper is normative Christian practice. It was a central principle of the Anglican reformers of the 16th century, enshrined in the first *Book of Common Prayer* and its successors down to the present. It is the assumed activity of Christian communities as a normal dimension of Sunday worship in the *Book of Alternative Services*.

For Christians well into the middle ages, the phrase 'the Body of Christ' evoked three images: the Body of Christ, risen ascended and glorified; the Body of Christ, broken and shared in the eucharist; the Body of Christ, men, women, and children reborn through the waters of baptism. These images were inseparable. They contributed a sense of wholeness to the eucharistic assembly and to the diverse ministries exercised by the whole people of God. As this unity of images began to dissolve, the sense that ministry was exercised by the whole community began to disintegrate and the liturgical celebration became increasingly clericalized to the exclusion of the active participation of the laity.

The celebration of the liturgy as found in the *BAS* invites the total participation of the people of God. The appropriate metaphor for the eucharist is therefore a community or family celebration in which all actively participate, rather than an activity performed by the ordained for a laity whose role has been reduced to that of observer. A community or family celebration takes on its fullest meaning when all participants are involved in the preparation as well as in the event itself.

In the celebration of the liturgy various ministers, both ordained and lay, are appointed for a variety of functions. Persons carry out their specific duties without usurping the responsibilities of the other ministers. In the tradition to which most of us have become accustomed, the ordained have assumed a diversity of ministries, both clerical and lay. It has been taken for granted that presiding, reading, leading the prayers, preparing the bread and wine, and distributing communion were all inherently clerical functions, and that (with the exception of choir and servers) lay participation was confined to the pews. The rediscovery of the original diversity of ministries within the celebration of the liturgy is one of the exciting aspects of renewal in the churches today. So too, the diversity of participants, ordained and lay, male and female, young and old, help us to rediscover the wholeness of the people of God. The celebration of the liturgy is the privilege, obligation, and function of all the leaders of worship jointly. It is the presider's duty and joy to encourage this spirit in the leaders, and gently to guide their actions so that everything will be done to assist God's people to worship with confidence and eagerness.

In keeping with the renewed understanding of the eucharist the word 'presider' has been used in this book to describe the person presiding over the eucharistic assembly. The term 'president' dates from early Christian times; it appears in the *Epistle to the Magnesians* (6; c. 105 A.D.) of Ignatius of Antioch (c. 110) and in Justin's (c. 155) *First Apology* (65:3,5; 67:5 c. 155 A.D.). Its use has created negative cultural reactions in Canada. The term 'presiding celebrant' was intended to suggest that the whole people of God celebrates the eucharist together, and not that an ordained person performs for those assembled. It is important to recall that the person presiding acts not so much *in persona Christi* (in the person of Christ) but *in nomine ecclesiae* (in the name of the gathered community). Since the *BAS* rites took shape, 'presider' has come to be accepted increasingly as an accurate description of the role of liturgical presidency, while escaping the more awkward 'presiding celebrant'.

If the liturgy is to help us become what God calls us to be, it must reflect the life to which the community is called so that we may know who we are and who we can become. This view of the liturgical text as a means to the self-articulation of the life of a parish implies a quite different appreciation of the purpose and function of the text than that which has been common.

One of the factors leading to liturgical revision in the past was reflection on the shape of the liturgy. As a result there have been a diversity of local revisions some of which have been ill-informed. It is important to remember that each rite in the *BCP* and *BAS* possesses its own integrity. In giving us these rites the Church has carefully balanced the inherited historical tradition and contemporary pastoral needs. To interpolate additional texts, rearrange elements, or omit portions randomly, often upsets the pastoral and theological balance of the rites themselves.

Many of the contemporary rites do not include some elements which, over the years, have won a place for themselves in popular piety. Elements such as the Prayer of Humble Access and the Comfortable Words have been retained in the Holy Eucharist (1962) in the *BAS*. To interpolate elements such as these into the modern language rite is inappropriate to the shape and integrity of the rite itself.

To engage in liturgical renewal and to develop a new rite is not merely the changing of words but the formation of a new piety. To do everything as we have always done it and only to change the words is to misunderstand the nature of liturgical renewal. These changes call upon all liturgical ministers, but especially those who preside over the eucharistic assembly, to rethink each action in the light of the new rite. Ways of organizing the liturgical space, the preparation of the altar, manual gestures of presiders, and the activities of servers and other ministers, lay and ordained, need to change. This is so because what we do speaks as loudly as what we say in liturgy. Actions need to support and reflect the words of the rite so that together they contribute to the wholeness of the liturgical celebration rather than creating a sense in which one struggles against or undermines the other. This renewal of liturgical piety which combines text, gesture, posture, liturgical space, vesture, movement and song is the real challenge which lies at root of renewed liturgical community.[1]

On Posture

Christian worship is not just a cerebral activity. The true worship of God involves our whole selves: body, mind and spirit. Consequently, how we use our bodies in worship is important. Traditionally, Anglicans are accustomed to a variety of postures for worship. We have tended to stand to sing, to sit to listen, and to kneel to pray. As parishes renew their worship, they will want to reflect on posture and the theological statements various postures make during the course of a liturgical celebration. In this reflection, insights from the Church's past can be helpful.

For many Anglicans standing to pray is a novelty. But from the days of the early church up until the middle ages, Christians were forbidden to kneel for public prayer on Sundays and during Eastertide. Sunday, the Lord's Day, is a weekly celebration of the resurrection. In baptism, Christians die in the Lord and are raised to new life with him. For centuries this theological reality was expressed in the posture of the faithful. Standing was seen as a sign that they had died to sin and were now risen to share the life of the risen Lord. It was a sign of solidarity with him and with each other in that risen life. Standing is also a sign of the community's solidarity in the celebration of the liturgy as a whole. As we are all celebrants of the eucharist, assuming a posture different from that of the presider implies that the liturgy is something the presider is doing for the faithful rather than something the community does together.

Kneeling in worship was reserved for particular times of the year. It was a particular sign of penitence and was therefore a common posture during the season of Lent. Even then, however, only those who had been excommunicated or who were undergoing a long period of penitence, were directed to kneel on Sundays in Lent. Kneeling on Sundays became common only when there was a rigid separation between the liturgical activity of the clergy and laity in the Sunday celebration. The laity were reduced to passive spectators who attended to their own private prayers while the clergy and choir performed the actual liturgy itself. Our own reformers in the sixteenth century reacted against this privatized understanding of worship but were unable to move the church on the question of the physical position of the congregation or the penitential piety which inspired it.

---

[1] See D. Holeton, "The Formative Character of Liturgy" [Papers of the Second International Anglican Liturgical Consultation] in Thomas Talley ed. *A Kingdom of Priests: Liturgical Formation of the People of God* (Alcuin/GROW Liturgical Study 5) pp. 8-14.

Today, many parishes that have reflected on the question of posture and have changed from kneeling to standing for prayer have found that it has brought new insight into their understanding of public worship and of themselves as a community. When parishes engage in this discussion it is important to assure an openness to a diversity of postures. The elderly, for example, often find long periods of kneeling or standing difficult. They should be made to feel free to assume the posture in which they are most comfortable. Similarly standing to receive communion is often much easier for some elderly people. They should not be made to feel that not kneeling at the altar rail is a gesture in some way lacking reverence.

Standing, kneeling or sitting, are not the only questions which need reflection when a community comes to consider the issue of posture during the liturgy. These postures themselves are susceptible to a great variety of permutations. For example, there is a difference in how we might stand while listening to the proclamation of the Gospel and how we might stand in prayer during the Great Thanksgiving. In the later, it would be appropriate for the whole congregation to raise their arms in the biblical posture associated with prayer, something which would be unusual during the Gospel reading.

As parish communities reflect on the renewal of their worship, reflection on posture and gesture will become an intrinsic part of that process. To change liturgical texts without reflecting on the context in which the texts are celebrated is to appropriate only part of liturgical renewal in which texts, posture, gesture, music and space constitute a whole.[2]

On Vesture

In what and how various liturgical ministers vest for the eucharist is not a matter of indifference. Vesture transmits messages about our understanding of baptism as the source of all Christian ministry, about the variety of ministries exercised in the liturgical assembly, about our understanding of Holy Order, about our concern for the place of beauty and art in the worship of God, as well as about our care of creation.

All ministry in the Church flows from our baptism when each Christian is consecrated a member of the royal priesthood. It is because of our baptism that each Christian is called to a ministry of service (*diaconia*) in the world. If all those who exercise a particular liturgical ministry are vested in a clerical or pseudo-clerical fashion, the common baptismal ministry of Christians is marred. We can understand this, perhaps, if we remember that the oldest vestment used

---

[2] A helpful resource to help communities reflect on posture and liturgy is *Gestures and Symbols* [National Bulletin on Liturgy 94 (May-June 1984)]. Available from: National Liturgical Office, 90 Parent Avenue, Ottawa, Ontario K1N 7B1.

in the Church was the white baptismal garment given to each new Christian at their baptism. Distinction of dress among the various orders of ministry is a much later phenomenon in the life of the Church. As every baptized Christian is a member of the royal priesthood, there are ministries exercised in the liturgical assembly by right of the dignity of our baptism alone. It is therefore inappropriate to insist that readers, those leading the Prayers of the People, or lay ministers of communion must appear in special liturgical vesture.

As liturgical vesture became common in the life of the Church, each of the three major orders (bishop, presbyter, and deacon) came to have their own distinct liturgical clothing. This distinctive clothing was a reflection of their respective order within the Christian community, orders which had their own particular liturgical ministry as well as their distinctive role within the community as a whole. Baptized Christians could be ordained directly to any of these orders without passing through a heirarchical sequence on the way. As such, there was no sense of collecting a variety of orders and no possibility of vesting in another's order. Bishops, for example, could not vest as deacons even if they had been one.

As the Church reflects on the restoration of the diaconate within its life, priests need to reflect on the damage they do to any attempt to restore the integrity of this ministry within the Anglican Church of Canada when they dress as deacons, rather than presbyters, in the liturgy. While, in the absence of a deacon, priests may exercise liturgical ministries which have historically been those of deacons (reading the Gospel, preparing the gifts etc.), they perform those ministries as priests and not as deacons.

Vesture, because it involves fabric and colour, is an area where the Church must be concerned with valuing the role played by beauty and art in the worship of God. While worship is no less "valid" if celebrated in cheap, ill-fitting or gaudy vesture, the use of such clothing makes a particularly strong statement about our care for the liturgy as a whole and our concern for offering the best of our human gifts and creativity to God. As parishes acquire new vestments, they should make a serious effort to find artists who have the skill to produce vestments which are designed for the building in which they will be worn and for the size and shape of the person who will be wearing them. This is one way in which the Church can continue to exercise its responsibility in encouraging the gifts and talents of artists and using the best of human creativity for the worship of God.

Finally, our choice of vesture speaks of our concern for God's creation. Just as Percy Deamer chastised the Victorian church for its use of "sweated altars" (altars made in workshops in which the labourers were not paid a living wage) the Church in our own age needs to raise its consciousness about the materials used in its vestments and furnishings. For example, it is perhaps time that parishes made a conscious effort to choose natural fibres which are friendly to the environment rather than synthetic fabrics which are known to be created through processes which are detrimental to the environment. A conscious effort to use natural fibres in the Church's vesture makes an important statement about the interplay between human activity and the created order and the eucharist as the locus at which all of creation is brought together and offered to God.

On Liturgical Space

It is not possible within the context of this booklet to deal adequately with the question of liturgical space. As many congregations move into liturgical renewal, more and more of them are discovering that the liturgical space which they have inherited is not adequate for their present liturgical needs. This is largely because liturgical renewal has brought new insights into the nature of liturgical celebration. This centres largely on the rediscovery of the place of baptism in the life of the community, the centrality of the Sunday Eucharist and its character as the communal meal, and the renewed understanding of ministry within the Church in which the baptismal ministry of all the People of God, clergy and laity alike, is affirmed during the eucharistic celebration.

The consequences of these theological insights involve a major re-orientation of liturgical space. Since baptism is incorporation into the body of Christ which is manifested by the local community, baptisms must be held when the entire community is gathered and not privately, in the absence of the worshipping community, as was the case so often in the past. The font needs to be given a more central position where it is clearly visible to the whole community. Similarly, since the weekly Eucharistic gathering is our ongoing response to the covenant made in baptism, the font needs to be clearly visible to the members of the community as they enter the place where they will celebrate the eucharist. Since baptism is death and burial with Christ and new birth in him, the font itself must be capable of bearing the symbolic weight of those two actions. It is only with the most vivid of imaginations that a community can see this taking place when most of our fonts can barely contain enough water to dampen foreheads, let alone bear the images of tomb and womb. In the light of this many communities are re-considering not only the place of the font, but its size, shape and capacity to use "living water."

As the majority of Canadian parishes have rediscovered the centrality of the weekly eucharist and the importance of the eucharistic meal to the nurture of the whole community, the character and position of the Lord's Table has become an important consideration. The altar bears at least two important symbolic images. It is both a table, around which the whole community can gather for the meal at which the Lord is host and to which we are invited, as well as an altar on which we offer our pure sacrifice of praise and thanksgiving.

These two images must be allowed to live in a certain tension. In many of our parish churches we have allowed the image of altar to dominate that of table. It is important that we redress this imbalance. Consequently, many parishes are finding that an altar, removed to the extreme end of the building around which there can be little sense of their corporate gathering, does not adequately express the role of the whole community in celebrating the eucharistic meal. Simply moving the altar a few feet from the east wall so that the priest can celebrate facing the people is an inadequate resolution to the spacial demands engendered by the need for a sense of communal gathering at the table.

The Church's reflection on our common baptismal ministry has brought many communities to challenge the messages transmitted by the traditional arrangement in liturgical space in which there are clearly delineated areas for the clergy and laity. As a wider variety of the community exercise liturgical ministries in the Sunday assembly and do not vest in a clerical fashion to do so (eg. readers, communion ministers) this separation of liturgical space is much more visually evident. Consequently, communities are reflecting on how to arrange their liturgical space so that a reader going from the congregation to the lectern or the place from which communion will be distributed is not clearly a visual violation of "clerical space."

Finally, the place from which the 'gathering of the community' and 'the proclamation of the word' are presided is one which can be particularly difficult in the spaces we have inherited. It is important that the presider and assistants be clearly visible to the whole congregation as this is an intrinsic part of liturgical presidency. At the same time this place needs to be distinct from the place at which the eucharist is celebrated - the altar. Ideally, this might be to the side of the altar space so that liturgy of word and table are not presided from places on a single axis. Because many of our inherited buildings are narrow rectangular spaces, this is often not possible. In these situations, the sight lines themselves dictate a single axis unless the architectural integrity of the building is to be seriously violated. Congregations finding themselves in this situation often find that the best solution for the arrangement of liturgical space is to bring the altar well forward (best to the crossing, if there is one) and to place the presider and assistants sufficiently behind so that there is a visual separation between the two places of presiding. (Diagram 1)

In arranging the space for presiding at the liturgy of the word, attention must be paid to the way in which the presider's book, or sacramentary, will be used. Ideally, the book is brought out and held by a server or other assisting minister for the variable prayers. If a community does not have sufficient human resources to provide someone for this particular ministry a small, unobtrusive lectern to hold the sacramentary can be placed in front of the presider's chair. In either case, it is important that the presider's hands are free for the appropriate gestures of greeting and prayer and not incumbered with a book.

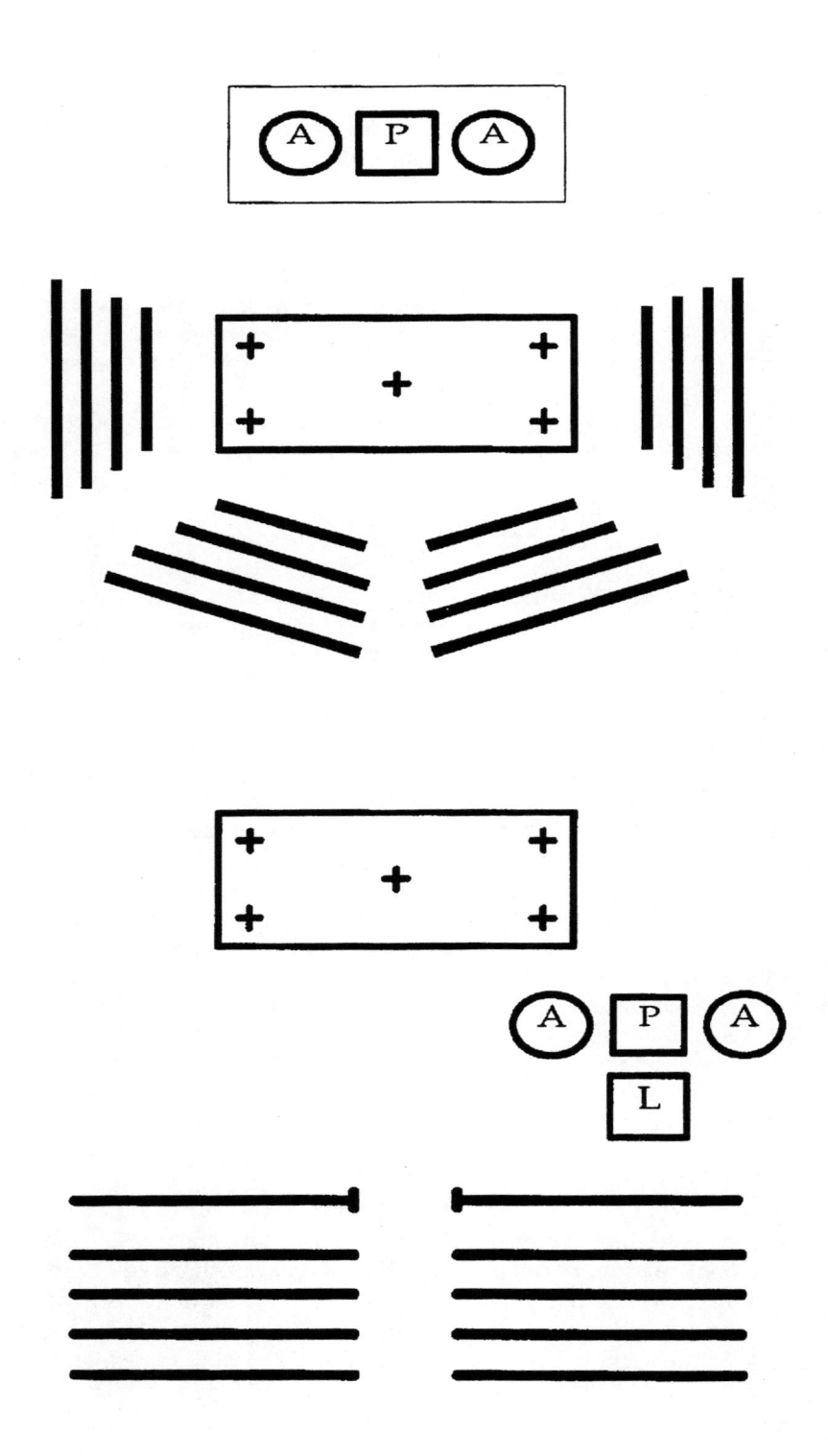

Legend: P = Presider   A = Assistant   L = Lectern

Diagram 1

In making any changes to liturgical space, sensitivity to the existing architecture is important in order to avoid creating spatial incongruities which can be the source of ongoing congregational friction. It is important to remember that, because any church building has been the site of important rites of passage for many members of the community (eg. marriage, the burial of a spouse or dead child), there is strong emotional attachment to existing liturgical space. In raising questions of liturgical space it is important to help congregations identify and value these emotional feelings about their worship space, rather than allowing them to go unaddressed and to surface as a negative element in the process of renewal. Any change of liturgical space will involve a certain amount of emotional reaction. Consequently, the renewal of liturgical space should involve careful planning by wide representation of community members and with a sensitivity to the emotions involved.

CHAPTER 1
PREPARATION FOR
THE LITURGY

The celebration of the eucharist calls upon all present to be active participants in the liturgy. The congregation can be called to a greater degree of participation first by encouraging the people to share responsibility for planning their own liturgical life. Every parish needs to work towards having both a worship committee and worship planning teams. Worship committees should eventually be composed of members who represent a variety of interests in the parish community. For example, representatives of each liturgical community (eg. 8:00, 9:15, 11:00 if there are several), members of servers, altar guild, choir, ushers, parish council, etc.. Its purpose is to set goals for the liturgical activity of the parish as a whole. After some study of the general principles of worship[3] the committee might consider such issues as frequency of service times, renewal of liturgical space, models for preparation for baptism, and similar matters. Liturgical planning teams share in the ongoing planning and evaluation of particular liturgies. Working within the general guidelines and goals established by the worship committee, planning committees need to be given the freedom to organize the actual content of Sunday worship. Only those who are actual members of a particular liturgical community can participate in these planning groups as it would be inappropriate for members of other communities to impose their ideas on a community in which they do not participate. These groups can only be successful when ongoing education and study in the area of liturgical life are a part of their programme.

Greater congregational participation can be assured by the planning committee overseeing the weekly resources for liturgy. A carefully designed pew leaflet provides all the information normally needed for full participation in the liturgy. Announcements of liturgical directions during the course of the liturgy are distracting and disrupt the flow of the liturgy itself. Accordingly, if variations from the usual order or any new music are to take place, they must be carefully introduced a few minutes before the service begins. It is important to recognize that when a particular rite is used consistently, week by week, congregations quickly learn the shape of the liturgy and do not need constant reminding of page numbers and other regular elements of the service. When the ability of the congregation to take responsibility for its own participation in the liturgy

---

[3] A good beginning could be Charles Price and Louis Weil, *Liturgy for Living* (Anglican Book Centre: Toronto 1979) and James C. Fenhagen, Use Guide for Liturgy for Living (The Seabury Press: New York 1979).

is respected, people are free to focus their attention on the work of worship, the service flows smoothly, and the liturgy takes on vitality and freedom.

Those who will participate in the leadership of the liturgy in the role of server, reader, intercessor, communion administrator, or musician must be thoroughly prepared for the tasks they will undertake. Each participant needs to understand the importance and significance of his or her role in the context of the whole liturgy. General training and regular rehearsal, rather than being merely formalistic, enable liturgical ministers to become sufficiently secure and relaxed with their tasks and should be a regular feature of liturgical preparation. This allows both the liturgical minister and the whole community to worship without being distracted by the anxieties of those who have not been adequately prepared for their ministries.

Servers should know their roles well and be capable of quiet, alert attention and prompt response to the needs of the participants in the liturgy. Readers need to have training to enable them to make themselves clearly heard and understood in the liturgical assembly. If microphones and lectern lights are used, readers need to be familiar with this equipment in order to minimize awkward fumbling. Readers, as stewards of God's word, must prepare the reading carefully so that scripture may be proclaimed intelligently and intelligibly.

Intercessors also need to learn to use their voices so as to be clearly heard and understood. Leading the prayers of the people is a demanding role, guidance and resources for the task will need to be provided.

In addition to musical rehearsals, musicians should work toward a deeper understanding of the role of music in the liturgy and the importance of timing. As a part of their preparation for the regular meetings of the liturgical planning committee, musicians must develop a particular awareness of the theological significance of the hymnody and other music selected for the service. This is important because the choice of hymns and other liturgical music should be made by the planning team as a whole.

Presiding at a contemporary eucharist is in many ways unlike celebrating in the past. Because revised rites assure a diversity of liturgical ministries, presiders must share many of their former tasks with others. But in sharing these tasks the presider does not abandon responsibility for the coherence of the liturgy as a whole. To preside well is to affirm and nurture the ministries of others, which means that presiders need to be aware of each participant, ensuring that each is present and prepared. A glance or a slight nod might be necessary to provide a cue or encouragement during the liturgy. Presiders, by their attitude and bearing, can instill confident and worshipful attention in other liturgical ministers and the gathered community. A presider who is nervous or ill at ease will communicate uncertainty to all. This means that presiders must have an intimate knowledge of the liturgy as a whole and of each its constituent parts in order to support the function of assistant ministers, enable the participation of the people, and respond to any unforseen need.

The celebration of the eucharist requires much more thought and preparation than has been customary in most parishes using the *Book of Common Prayer*. Preparation, as has been discussed, begins days and weeks before with training, rehearsal, reflection, the writing of the Prayers of the People, the preparation of homilies, the baking of bread, etc. so that on the Sunday all the preparation culminates in the parish celebration when this diversity of ministry finds its unity in the eucharistic celebration.

On the Lord's Day, all who have a part in the leadership of worship should gather well in advance of the time of the celebration. This will assure the completion of all necessary preparations before the people assemble.

Great care needs to be taken to ensure that all books required for the service are marked and in place for each participant. The presider must also take time to prepare the sacramentary (Presider's book), locating the proper for the day and the eucharistic prayer that has been chosen. Other important page turns also need to be marked, such as the Creed (if its to be used), the Lord's Prayer, etc..

Vessels and linen required for the celebration should be placed on the credence table and bread and wine sufficient for the needs of the community should be placed on an oblations table part way down the central aisle, or at the rear of the church. If there is to be a basket for contributions to a food bank, this should be placed beside the oblations table. Vestments should be laid out or hung in a convenient place and extra supplies of linen, bread, wine and other necessities should be readily available in a place well known to each server.

Chapter 1 - *Preparation for the Liturgy*

CHAPTER 2
THE GATHERING OF THE COMMUNITY

Some Historical Reflections on the Entrance Rite

One of the most unexamined aspects of our liturgies is what remains of the entrance rite. Historically we have various bits and pieces that have come to us from a variety of traditions. They need not all be used every Sunday. What is to take place during the entrance rite must be examined very closely, particularly in the context of the nature of a congregation and the time of the church year.

The Prayer Book entrance rite is the conflation of an elaborate tradition inherited form the Papal court and its dissemination throughout western Europe, together with private prayers of preparation for the priest derived from the Sarum use in England, and additional hortatory material inserted by the Reformers. All of this should not be used every Sunday.

The Collect for Purity is perhaps the best example of a vestigial "bit" in the entrance rite. Its original use was as part of the priest's private preparation in the Mediaeval Sarum rite. It also appears as the opening prayer in the mediaeval English devotional work *The Cloud of Unknowing*. When the prayer, in its English translation, was incorporated into the Prayer Book it remained a private devotional prayer for the celebrant. The Canadian Prayer Book (1962) is the first book used in this country in which the rubric required the prayer to be said aloud. In recent years it has become the custom in some parishes for the priest and people to say the prayer together.

While no one would doubt the place this prayer has won for itself in Anglican piety, the place it occupies in the liturgy is problematic. While its optional use is permitted by the rubrics, the tone and content of the prayer are in marked contrast to the shape and purpose of the gathering of the community. Presiders could perhaps consider using the prayer in its original context as a prayer of preparation before the liturgy begins. It could also become a part of the laity's preparation for the eucharist at home before they come to the eucharistic gathering. To use it as a part of the gathering of the community can inadvertantly introduce a liturgical piety which is in marked contrast to the community and celebratory qualities of renewed eucharistic piety.

Shape and Purpose Today

The purpose of the opening rite is to unite the assembled people as a community, to prepare them to listen to God's word and to enter into the eucharistic celebration. The gathering will best serve its intended purpose when its basic form varies with the liturgical season and time of year. On festivals such as Christmas and Easter it would appropriately assume a certain richness that contrasts vividly with a preparatory or penitential season or with an ordinary Sunday that has preceded it. In Lent or Advent it may be characterized by a certain simplicity or sobriety. On a quiet Sunday, for example in mid-summer, it would be appropriate to use the simplest form possible. The tenor of the whole liturgy that is to follow depends to a great extent on the mood that has been established in the opening rite. The normal shape for the Gathering of the Community in the eucharist has three basic elements: greeting, song of praise, and prayer (the Collect of the Day). While variations on this shape have their place for given days and seasons, these must be seen as exceptions to the normative pattern as described. What is said in the following pages about hymns before the greeting, announcements, litanies, the penitential rite or the Collect for Purity must be understood in that light.

Beginning the Service

It may seem strange to begin by talking about announcements, but this is perhaps the best place to begin. The difficulty with which announcements are integrated into the liturgy indicate that they are intrusions rather than a natural element of the liturgy. There are difficulties with almost every place at which announcements can occur. For example, to interpolate the announcements between gospel and sermon diminishes the integrity of the proclamation of the word in which scripture and sermon constitute an integral whole. Similarly, to place the announcements just before the service ends is often a glaring anticlimax.

An appropriate place for the community announcements is before the celebration itself begins. A person appointed can make the necessary announcements (not simply rehearsing the items in the bulletin) and other members of the community could be invited to add their own.

If there is new music, a brief time of rehearsal for the whole congregation might follow the community announcements. Care must be taken that these rehearsals do not take on disproportionate length and evolve into a liturgy in themselves.

Then the presider or an assistant may make any necessary liturgical announcements, making reference to the liturgical calendar, introducing the service, and explaining any variations in it. So that the announcements and any rehearsal are not seen as fixed liturgical element, a space of silence for reflection and gathering of thoughts between the last of the announcements and the entrance of the liturgical ministers and choir or the formal greeting by the presider is an appropriate part of the preparation for the celebration.

The Entrance

The route of the procession may vary depending on the nature of the building, the Sunday, or the day. In some places, because of cramped space or the shape of the building, indoor processions are rarely or never appropriate. In such places the service begins when all are assembled and the presider, already in his or her place, stands to greet the people. On days that are not festivals the entrance procession can proceed simply from the sacristy or rear of the nave to the chairs for the ministers. On festivals a long procession may be appropriate. It could proceed, for example, from the chancel, down the centre aisle, around the church and then back down the centre aisle into the chancel. (Diagram 2)

If there is a procession it is appropriate that it be led by servers carrying a cross and lighted tapers. The book of the Gospels, a book of appropriate size and dignity, may be carried in the entrance procession, and placed on the altar. The book is carried upright, at at least chest height or held aloft. Torches might also be carried on either side of it. The book is so honoured because as an acknowledgement of the presence of Christ who speaks to us in the Gospel.

After reverencing the altar, the ministers go to their places facing the congregation. This is the place from which the presider presides over the liturgy of the word. The altar is not yet the focus of attention. The place of liturgical presidency must be in full view of the congregation so that the presider can have visual contact with the gathered assembly. In most parishes this involves a rethinking of the arrangement of liturgical space. (See "On Liturgical Space", p. vi.)

The Greeting

The presider, standing at the chair, makes visual contact with the people and greets them with the Apostolic greeting: "The grace of our Lord Jesus Christ, and the love of God and the fellowship of the Holy Spirit be with you." The sign of the cross is not made by either presider or congregation. This is because the purpose of the greeting is to establish a relationship between the presider and the community. A gesture which focuses on the individual rather than the communal relationship detracts from the purpose of this element in the liturgy. (This contrasts with the American Episcopal rite where the sign of the cross might appropriately accompany the acclamation which is not intended to serve

Diagram 2

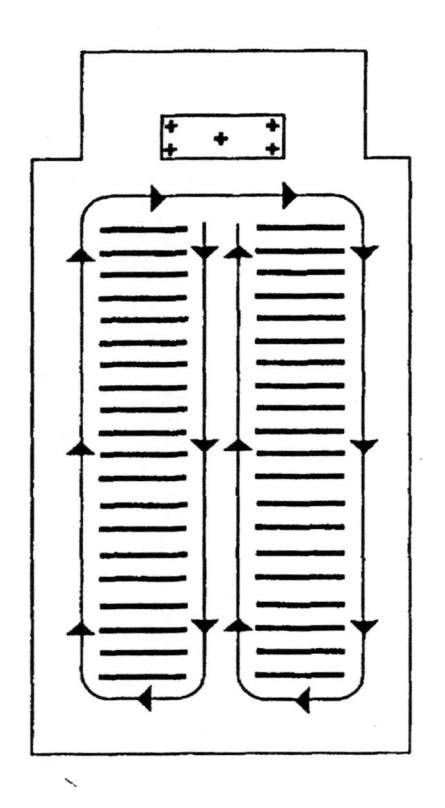

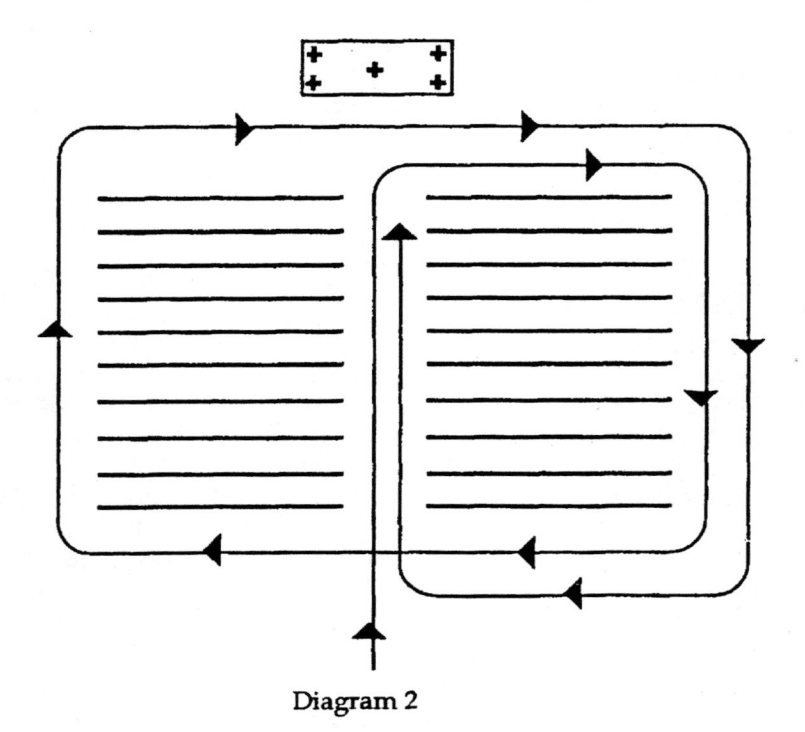

Chapter 2 - *The Gathering of the Community*

as a greeting.) The presider's hands should be open in welcome toward the people as he or she says the Greeting. (Diagram 3)

During the great Fifty Days, that is from Easter Day until Pentecost, a seasonal greeting is appointed: "Alleluia Christ is risen; the Lord is risen, indeed, Alleluia. May his grace and peace be with you; may he fill our hearts with joy." This greeting alone is to be used during Eastertide and is not simply to be added to the Apostolic greeting.

Song of Praise

The rubrics direct that a song of praise may be sung after the greeting. This is to provide a vigorous, unified congregational action to begin the service. Communal song is one of the most binding of human activities. Many voices blend into one common, ordered, offering of praise to God.

The music at this point helps set the character of the entire celebration. Therefore, the choice of music should reflect the readings of the day and the season of the church year. On ordinary Sundays this could be a hymn that picks up one of the themes that will be found in the readings or prayers. During the Easter or Christmas season and on festivals, the Glory to God is appropriate. A metrical version might be sung if musical possibilities are limited or if the congregation does not know a setting of the ICET text. If other resources are not available, because this text is inherently musical in nature, settings of the Prayer Book text may also be used.

The *Gloria in Excelsis* was originally a part of the daily prayer of the church and was imported from there into the eucharist. It was never intended to be the invariable feature of the eucharist that our practice has often assumed it to be. It is therefore, perhaps most appropriately reserved for festivals, as was the practice when it first appeared in the celebration of the eucharist. At the same time, congregations may find that there are hymns that capture the joy and spirit of a particular festival in a more immediate fashion than does the Glory to God. In that case it would be better to sing the hymn.

Lent may be an appropriate season to use the Kyrie. While in its origin the Kyrie was often a litany response and not a penitential text, it has become closely associated with penitence in many people's minds. Various musical settings have done much to reinforce this. If a litany were to be sung at the entrance, 'Kyrie eleison' or 'Lord have mercy' could be used as the congregation's response to each petition. This would restore the refrain to its original liturgical context. In this case, the litany would appropriately end with the collect of the day. This form of litany and collect would replace *all* other parts of the entrance rite on that day.

The Trisagion is unfamiliar to most Anglicans. It therefore has not acquired

Diagram 3

Chapter 2 - *The Gathering of the Community*

particular seasonal connotations. It could become a part of the usual Sunday liturgy, leaving the Kyrie for Lent, and the Glory to God for festive seasons. If it were to be given seasonal character, it could possibly become a feature of the Advent liturgy.

In parishes where there has been a tradition of singing canticles at the Offices, the use of a canticle here could maintain that tradition and provide a pastoral means of introducing those who are accustomed to the Sunday Office to the spirit of this rite. The *Book of Alternative Services* provides a great variety of canticles as well as suggestions for seasons in which various canticles are appropriate (pp. 72-74). This would be a valuable resource for parishes who wish to draw on this rich tradition.

While most congregations will prefer to explore the rich variety of musical resources which have been written for the new liturgical texts the preface to the *BAS* (p.13) reminds us that the new book "is intended to extend, not break, the tradition of the Church, and not least in the area of music". The `Glory to God', `Kyrie Eleison', `Trisagion', `Holy, Holy, Holy', `Lamb of God' and canticles play a role comparable to that of hymns, and as such they may continue to be sung to settings, and with words, that are a part of the parish's musical tradition. It is generally preferable to keep the traditional words to the traditional tunes than to try to make the new words fit the old music.

The Collect

The presider says or sings: "Let us pray", and allow a space of silence during which the community may pray silently. When this silence is first introduced, the parish community may mistakenly interpret "Let us pray" to mean "Please kneel", but a change of posture at this particular point would be inappropriate. For a while the presider may have to say: "As we remain standing, let us pray".

After a short silence, the presider opens his or her hands in the classic attitude of prayer (See Diagram 3). The Collect of the Day is a presidential prayer, and consequently there is no provision for the congregation to pray the prayer in unison. Just as it is inappropriate for the presider to usurp the liturgical ministries of others, so too it is inappropriate for others to usurp texts which are specifically those of the presiding celebrant.

Only one collect is used. The rubrics intentionally make no provision for the repetition of seasonal collects as does the *Book of Common Prayer*. It is the purpose of the Collect as a single act of prayer to "collect" the prayers of the community and bring the gathering rite to a conclusion. (If, on a weekday, several saints are being commemorated on one day, the collect of one of the saints should be used, the other commemorations should either be included in the Prayers of the People or omitted altogether.)

After the presider has finished the collect, the people say or sing, "Amen", and are then seated to listen to the first reading.

Models for the Gathering of the Community

Seasonal Models

The following models are a guide to the various ways in which the Gathering of the Community might be used so that it might achieve its intended purpose.

    Ordinary Sundays
        1.
        Greeting
        Hymn
        Collect of the Day
        2.
        Greeting
        Canticle appropriate to the season
        Collect of the Day
        3.
        Greeting
        Collect of the Day

    Easter Season
        Hymn in procession
        Easter Greeting
        Glory to God
        Collect of the Day

    Christmas Season
        Hymn in Procession
        Greeting
        Glory to God
        Collect of the Day

Lent
> 1.
> Greeting
> Kyrie
> Collect of the Day
> 2.
> Penitential Order
> Collect of the Day
> 3.
> Litany in procession (*BAS* p. 110 or a similar litany with appropriate interpolations) concluding with the Collect of the Day instead of the collect on p. 111.

Advent
> 1.
> Greeting
> Trisagion
> Collect of the Day
> 2.
> Greeting
> Advent Hymn or Canticle
> Collect of the Day

Festivals
> as at Christmas

Weekdays or other 'said' services
> Greeting
> Collect of the Day

A Penitential Order

A Penitential Order (pp. 216-17) may be used in the season of Lent in two different ways: either as a separate liturgy before the gathering of the community, or as the gathering of the community. If the penitential order is used before, it may follow the announcements of the day before the service begins. To do this the presider, vested, enters alone from the side with the others who would be in the procession waiting at the back. When the penitential order is over, a space of silence is observed while the presider joins the others in the procession for the entrance. Since the greeting will have already been used in the penitential order, the presider will want to consider whether it is appropriate to greet the community a second time after the entrance or, instead, to begin with the Collect of the Day.

When the penitential order takes the place of the usual gathering of the commu-

The Gathering of the Community - Chapter 2

nity, the procession enters in silence or accompanied by quiet music and the ministers take their usual places and begin the penitential order. After the absolution, the community could sing a hymn of praise which would be followed by the Collect of the Day. This then constitutes the gathering of the community for the day and the Proclamation of the Word follows.

When the penitential order is used as an antecedent to the liturgy the confession and absolution which may otherwise follow the Prayers of the People are not used. The penitential petition in the Prayers of the People is omitted also in this case.

CHAPTER 3
PROCLAMATION OF THE WORD

The Lectionary in the BAS

The Lectionary in the *BAS* uses a three year cycle of readings based on *The Common Lectionary* which has seen widespread ecumenical acceptance. The basic structure is three readings and a Psalm or portion of a Psalm at each Sunday celebration. The use of this lectionary assures that over the three year cycle more of the scriptures, particularly the Old Testament, is covered in readings than has ever been the case in the eucharist in the past.

Preparation for Readers

In the proclamation of the word the Christian community retells its story, reflects on the word of God to our forebears in faith, and listens to discern the word of God to the Christian community today. It is important that we recapture the sense of listening as a corporate act as opposed to individual reading. This can be facilitated when readings are clearly and intelligibly proclaimed and can be diminished when lectionary leaflets or pew Bibles become an occasion for the individualization of the word of God. It is better to encourage people to read the texts before they come to worship, than it is to encourage them to follow the texts during the liturgy itself. Many parishes have discovered that publishing the readings for the following Sunday in the weekly bulletin has helped the community to hear the word of God more fruitfully and with greater understanding.

The first and second readings are normally read by lay persons who are members of the congregation. It is in their capacity as laypeople that they share in the proclamation of the word. Consequently it is important to guard against any apparent clericalization of this ministry. Dressed in ordinary clothing (the vesture of the laity), each reader comes up from the congregation to read and then returns to the congregation afterward.

Readers are persons who will be able to make themselves heard and understood in the liturgical assembly. It is important that training be offered for prospective readers and that there be some form of continuing support to readers in their ministry. Readers need to be scheduled and advised of the reading(s) and the biblical translation to be used well in advance of the date on which they read. They will then have time to prepare thoroughly for their role in the liturgy.

Readers may also need some general instruction about movement during the liturgy. Movement should be natural and unhurried, not stiff, formal or hasty. The task is important and time needs to be taken to perform it well. Readers need to be familiar and at ease with the lectern light and microphone. Any necessary adjustments to this equipment or to the lectern itself should be made, if possible, before the service begins.

The scriptures have within them the story of our faith. The book from which is read the record of God's self-revelation ought to be of imposing size and dignity. It is important to understand that the scriptures are the possession of the whole community and not of a particular individual. Therefore the text used is not an incidental matter, but is an important liturgical sign of the role scripture plays within the community. The use of pew leaflets, pocket or individual Bibles fails to recognize the importance of this liturgical sign. The book to be used must be clearly marked for each reading well in advance of the start of the service to avoid any awkward or embarrassing fumbling with the book.

The announcement of the reading is prescribed: "A reading from...." There is little need to specify the verses read since that information is secondary to the content of the reading, and the announcement can be cumbersome when the reading is drawn from two chapters and verses are skipped. Verses placed in parenthesis in the lectionary may be omitted in public reading if a briefer reading is desired. These verses form part of the reading however, and are recommended for the preacher's consideration.

In order to avoid confusion for listeners some clarification of the reading may need to be provided by the reader. For example, if the speaker is not identified in the beginning of a reading, or if the antecedent of a pronoun is not clear, readers should replace the pronoun with the noun. "He said to him" becomes "Moses said to Pharaoh". Or a phrase may be added identifying the speaker, ("Joshua said" or "Jeremiah writes"). Many readings, particularly from the Gospels, need a preface ("Jesus said" or "At that time Jesus said") in order to make sense. Temporal references which add nothing to the meaning and which may distract the congregation's attention from the content may be eliminated (e.g."Jesus said" instead of "After that Jesus said"). The reader should pause briefly after announcing the reading and before beginning the reading. This allows the congregation to prepare to hear the reading itself.

At the end of the reading there should be a brief but distinct pause before the reader, looking up at the congregation, says, "The word of the Lord." As at the beginning of the reading, the pause detaches the reading from the invitation to respond and allows the reading to come to a natural conclusion in the listeners' mind before they are asked to respond. Looking up at the congregation indicates that the response is a brief dialogue between the reader and the congregation, and not a part of the reading itself. For the same reason the reader should make no motion to leave the lectern until the people have responded, "Thanks be to God".

The First Reading

After the Collect of the Day a reader goes to the place of reading and announces the first reading. Except on the Sundays of Easter, the first reading is from the Old Testament. The Hebrew people are the forebears and faith companions of Christians, and because of this relationship we continue to benefit from the Hebrew Scripture. A period of silence is appropriate following the first and second readings. Here, as in other places where silence is enjoined by the rubrics, it is important to understand silence as a corporate, rather than individual, activity. The community as a whole reflects on what they have heard in light of who they are as the People of God. When a period of silence is being observed, it would be helpful to the community as a whole if readers remained quietly at the place of reading until after the silence rather than returning to their place during the silence itself.

The Gradual or Meditation Psalm

A psalm is sung as a meditation on the first reading, as a response to it, and as a bridge to the second reading. The psalm is an important liturgical element. The required use of a psalm between the lections provides for the restoration of psalm singing to its traditional place in the life of the church and gives the worshipper the opportunity to participate in the singing of a portion of scripture, which is almost always a reflection on the first reading and offers significant spiritual insight on it. Psalms appointed for Sundays, festivals, and weekdays are included in the proper for each day. The psalm selection, like the gradual of some earlier liturgies, is not concluded with the Glory to the Father. The psalm prayers provided in the Psalter are intended for use in the Office but are not used with the psalm at the eucharist. Their function in the Office is to play the role of a meditation on the psalms but in the eucharist the psalm itself is the meditation. Because of the meditative quality of the psalm, sitting, rather than standing, is the appropriate posture.

The one quality which holds the psalter together is that all its texts were written to be sung. There are a wide variety of resources available to meet the needs of every parish. Some parishes may choose to continue singing psalms to chants which are familiar to the whole congregation (Anglican Chant, Plainsong). Many other congregations are finding that this is an ideal time to explore new ways of singing the psalms. A variety of publishers have made responsorial settings of the *BAS* Lectionary Psalms available and are proving themselves viable in parishes with widely varying musical capabilities. See Appendix 4.

The Second Reading

Immediately after the psalm, the second reading is announced and read. It is usually from a letter of one of the Apostles. It is read in the Christian assembly today just as it was once read in the midst of its first recipients. The announcement is prescribed, "A reading from...." The title of the book may be given simply, for example, "First Corinthians," rather than, "The first letter of St. Paul the Apostle to the Christians gathered at Corinth."

Brief introductions to these two readings are both appropriate and to be encouraged. They put the readings in a context so that the worshipper may listen with fuller understanding. In preparing these introductions it is important not to summarize the reading, but to put it in a context so that the hearers may listen more intelligently to the content of the reading itself. Summarizing the reading imposes an interpretive filter between the proclamation of scripture and those for whom it is read.

Music before the Gospel

The music used after the second reading and before the Gospel needs to be considered carefully. Its purpose is to prepare the community to hear the Gospel which is about to be proclaimed. Therefore, the music chosen should point the community towards the Gospel. This may be accomplished either by the choice of hymn, alleluia, or anthem. If a hymn is used it should not be divided in two so that some verses are sung before the Gospel and some after. There are a number of reasons for avoiding this practice. First, it violates the poetical integrity of the hymn itself. Further, sandwiching the reading in a hymn, allows the hymn to become central, rather than play a preparatory and supportive role. Finally, it creates an inappropriate block between Gospel and sermon.

The singing of an alleluia verse is another traditional way of preparing the community for the Gospel. A variety of musical resources for these are available. Some communities have found that the Sentence found at the beginning of each set of propers is an appropriate text for the alleluia verse. These are often sung by a cantor with the congregation singing well known alleluias (for example, from the hymn tunes *Lasst Uns Erfreuen, O filii et filiae, Vulpius,* or *Victory*) before and after the Sentence.

The Gospel

Historically, reading the Gospel is the privilege of the deacon. In the words of the Gospel, Christ comes to his people and speaks to them anew. This is the climax of scripture reading to which the first two readings point, and it is a principle way in which Christ is present in the eucharistic assembly. It is for this reason that the traditional posture for hearing the Gospel is standing, as a sign of respect for the personal presence of Christ. The reader first greets the community with the salutation, 'The Lord be with you', and then announces the Gospel as prescribed: "The Holy Gospel of our Lord Jesus Christ according to..." If the Gospel is sung, these acclamations are also sung.

The Gospel may be read either in the context of a gospel procession, or from the place of preaching. The purpose of the gospel procession is to bring the gospel into the midst of the congregation. It is accompanied by cross, candles, and possibly incense as a sign of respect for the presence of Christ. Because of this a number of liturgical ministers are involved in the procession. The procession begins during the music after the second reading when the crucifer and tapers (and possibly another assisting minister or server to hold the book during the reading) lead the reader into the midst of the congregation. As the procession moves to the centre of the congregation, the people turn to face the Gospel book, as an acknowledgement of the presence of Christ in the reading. It is important that the Crucifer is instructed to stop in the middle of the assembled people, rather than at a pre-determined spot so that, when few are present, the Gospel is not proclaimed in an empty space.

When the procession has reached the place of reading, the crucifer stops and turns to face back up the aisle. The tapers step aside to allow the person who will hold the book to come between them and stand with his or her back to the crucifer. The reader gives the book to the one that will hold it and opens it to the Gospel of the day. The tapers should be on either side of the book itself rather than on either side of the crucifer or reader. (Diagram 4)

Just as with the book used for the first and second readings, it is important that the book of the Gospels be of appropriate size and dignity.

At the conclusion of the Gospel reading, the reader raises the book so that it can be seen by the whole congregation and sings or says 'The Gospel of Christ'. After the congregation has made its response, the procession returns in the same order as it came. At this time church musicians could play appropriate instrumental music. Such music should be only of such duration and musical character as to cover the return of the Gospel procession and not so overshadow it that it becomes a musical interlude on its own.

The use of sung acclamations before and after the Gospel reading are vestiges

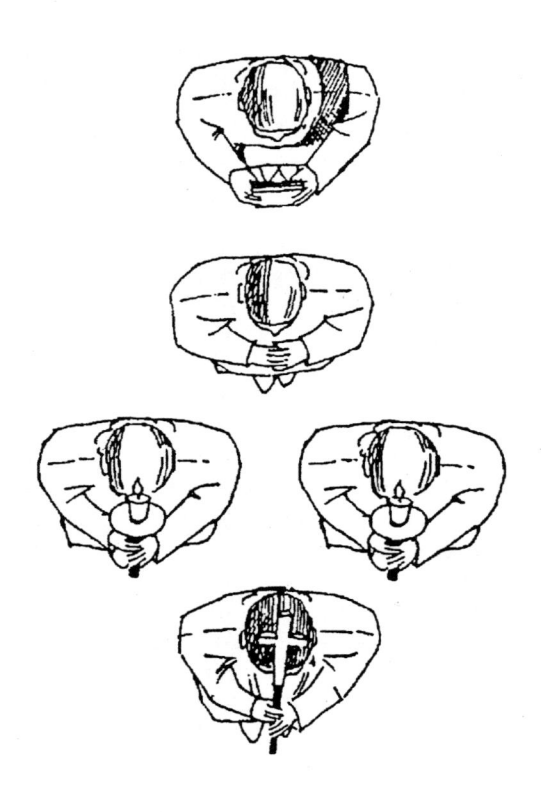

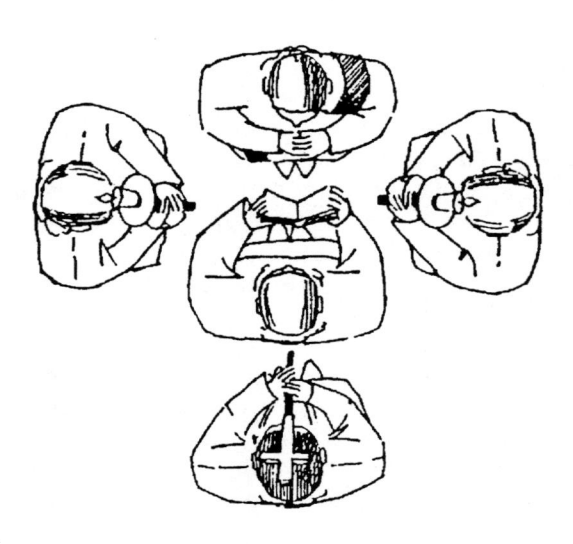

Diagram 4

Chapter 3 - *Proclamation of the Word*

from the time when the Gospel itself was sung. Communities may wish to consider the restoration of this practice, at least on major festivals and other occasions of particular solemnity. Many congregations have found that the singing of the Gospel can add a particular sense of the solemnity surrounding the proclamation of the Easter or Christmas Gospel. Information on ways in which the Gospel text (and other lections) can be noted and sung can be found on pp. 393-396 of the Presider's Edition of the *BAS*.

The Sermon or Homily

The sermon or homily is the living voice of the Gospel today. It is a normal part of the liturgy of the word on each Sunday and Holy Day. While in some places it has not been the custom to preach at "early" services on these days, a short homily is both appropriate and assumed as an integral part of the eucharist. It is the assumption of the *BAS* that preaching is a normative part of every eucharistic celebration.

The primary purpose of the sermon or homily in the liturgy is to reflect on the readings in such a way as to lead the congregation to praise and thanksgiving for what God has done and is doing in their lives and in the world. It should be the preacher's aim to shed light on the meaning of the scriptures for the day and show how they apply to the contemporary situation. In order to maintain the attention of the congregation and to preserve a balance between the elements of the liturgy, the length of the sermon needs to be planned with sensitivity. A silence for reflection is appropriate after the homily.

Creeds

The rubric directs that the creed may be said. It may also be omitted. It is normally omitted on weekdays, and it need not always be said on Sundays. The Nicene Creed might be reserved for use on more solemn or festive occasions. Following the original Greek text, the Nicene Creed has been translated with the plural pronoun, "We believe." The *BAS* provides the presider with an introductory line for both creeds so that the whole community can begin the actual recitation of the creed together. On occasion, the presider might introduce the recitation of the creed by relating it to the Gospel of the day or see it as a response to the homily.

The creed is a comparatively late addition to the liturgy, and has been traditionally regarded as an element that may be eliminated without damaging the integrity of the eucharistic rite. The eucharistic prayer, in any case, abounds in confessional and credal affirmations. If Holy Baptism, or another rite with a creed, is celebrated within the service, the creed is omitted at this point to avoid duplication. There are other occasions, like the Sunday of the Passion (Palm Sunday) where the length of the liturgy as a whole makes the elimination of a creed desireable. This is indicated in the rubrics for the day. On Sundays like Easter or Pentecost when the *BAS* encourages a corporate renewal of Baptismal vows (even when there is not a celebration of baptism) this would replace the use of the creed on that day.

Communities may need to rethink the posture assumed during the recitation of the creed. Turning eastward for the creed derived from the custom of celebrating the eucharist facing east. The *BAS* eucharistic rite assumes that the presider normatively faces the community. Turning toward the east for the recitation of the creed, when the eucharist is not celebrated in the eastward position, is an inappropriate gesture.

Musical settings of the creed may be used, but consideration needs to be given to the length of time required for the singing and also the nature of the text itself, posing the question of whether or not it is susceptible to musical settings accessible to the average congregation. It would be inappropriate for the creed to become an element of disproportionate weight in the context of the liturgy as a whole.

CHAPTER 4
PRAYERS OF THE PEOPLE

The prayers of the people are the response of the community to the proclamation of the word. They are a moment when the gathered community exercises its priestly role. Baptized into Christ, and made one in his body, we pray with Christ, the great high priest, who makes perpetual intercession for us and for all of creation. The Prayers of the People are also an initial step in a committment to action. While we pray for the world as we envision it perfected in Jesus Christ, our intercessions also need to be grounded in the present reality. For example, while a petition to "bring an end to all famine" is clearly grounded in the vision of the new creation, there is also an implicit demand that the Christian community make a tangible response to that petition. The petition would ring hollow if a community did not also respond in contributions to the local food bank, Primate's World Relief and a heightening of consciousness of the root problems perpetuating world hunger. So, at the same time, the prayers would appropriately include more specific petitions for the local situation. We cannot pray for something we ourselves are not prepared to become or to be involved in.

In the *BAS* the liturgical assembly is called to move from its reflection on God's word to response in an expression of thanksgiving and concern, naming in prayer, issues, both local and global, which are of current concern in the community. The prayers serve to provide focus and direction for the assembly. They are a response to the word proclaimed, they grow out of the context of the community and the content of the proclamation, and they prepare the people for the active response of the Christian life. In the prayers of the people the community is invited to enter actively into the work of worship.

The rubrics of the *BAS* anticipate either a deacon or lay person leading the Prayers of the People. A wide variety of forms and resources are provided by the book, but there is no intention that the person leading the prayers need feel limited to the resources provided. Those with responsibility for the ministry of leading prayer in the community must be sensitive, aware of the needs of the community and must take time for training and preparation for their task. There are many opportunities for creativity of expression but there are also many pitfalls to be avoided.

Preparation

In preparing the Prayers of the People, the intercessor should look at a variety of sources of material. Basic sources for the prayers arise from within the community itself and from the proclamation of the word. Intercessors may draw on the content of the readings for the day as a primary source for the prayers. The other major source is the intercessor's own awareness of issues of concern within the community and the world.

The prayers of the people are not intended to be used in a homiletical way. It is inappropriate for intercessors to use the prayers as a forum for their own agenda. It is in the posture of prayer that we, as a people of God, are most vulnerable to manipulation and coercion. Therefore, it is precisely at this time in our corporate life that the community stands in need of responsible, sensitive, leaders. Prayers of the people must be characterized by their inclusiveness and sensitivity.

The *BAS* provides a model for prayers on page 190. These categories need not *all* be included in the prayers each time the community gathers. They do, however, form a basic model which will give shape to the prayer.

Prayers of the People may take the form of a litany. Some examples of litanies which may be adapted for use according to the particular needs of the community appear on pages 110 to 128 of the *BAS*. A litany consists of a series of petitions sung or spoken by the leader to which the people respond with a fixed refrain. Most litanies can be sung; a sung litany is particularly appropriate on solemn and festive occasions. Some of the litanies provided in the *BAS* work well only if sung as they depend heavily on the musical cadence of the litany tone to give the congregation a "musical clue" when to respond. These litanies, if *said*, lead either to a slavish following of the printed text or to ragged entry on the refrain. When a litany is being sung, it is appropriate that at the end of the litany space be left for the prayers and thanksgivings of members of the congregation rather than interrupting the litany itself for spoken petitions. Musical resources for sung litanies may be found in the *BAS* on pages 915 to 917. If the singing of litanies is new to a community, it is often helpful to point the litany in advance and to provide copies for at least the cantor and choir.

On Sundays in Lent, a litany could be sung during the entry of either clergy and choir, or of the whole community. Care must be taken so that any additional concerns are included in the petitions. If a litany of this sort is used, the Prayers of the People are omitted from their usual place in the liturgy.

Eucharistic Prayer 6 provides opportunity for the inclusion of intercessory material. If extensive petitions are to be included in the Eucharistic Prayer itself, this takes the place of the Prayers of the People. While this is one option made possible by the *BAS*, its use should probably be infrequent and carefully considered.

Another form appropriate for the prayers of the people is a series of biddings, with or without collects. Whatever form is used for the prayers of the people, spaces of silence need to be provided to allow members of the community to add further petitions and thanksgivings. These spaces of silence may be left either at appropriate intervals throughout the prayers or the leader may add at the end of the final bidding or petition, "I bid your further intercessions and thanksgivings." The prayers may then be brought to a close by the use of a concluding collect.

In order to guide and direct the prayers of the church appropriately the intercessor needs to consider a number of important issues in the preparation and delivery of the prayers. One problem frequently encountered is the often excessive length of the prayers. It is important that the prayers do not overshadow the other elements of the liturgy by their length.

It is not necessary to pray for *every* concern in the parish each time the community gathers. Many of the issues of concern not mentioned by the intercessor will be raised by others in their petitions during the spaces of silence. Exhaustive prayers tend to preclude these petitions and defeat the sense that these are prayers *of the people*. We must also assume in our corporate life that we will worship together over an extended period of time; to attempt to include all our needs in one intercessory prayer tends to undermine this.

An approach some parishes find satisfactory is to establish a cycle of prayer for parish ministries, including both lay and clerical. Week by week a variety of ministries are upheld in prayer before God, bringing each ministry to mind in a more significant way than a more general prayer for lay and clerical leadership would allow.

It is appropriate that each Sunday the community pray for the Diocesan Bishop with whom they are in communion. It is through their bishop that the community is in communion with their Metropolitan, the Primate and the larger Church. Therefore the diocesan bishop is named *before* the Metropolitan, Primate or other church leaders.

Every care must be taken to ensure that the prayers are not exclusive. If, for example, one of the parish clergy is mentioned by name all should be included in the petition. It may be more appropriate to pray for "clergy, lay leaders, and people of the parish" rather than singling out one ministry alone for special mention unless all ministries are prayed for on a regular cycle.

A penitential petition is included in the prayers only after consulting the presider. It is not necessary to have both a penitential petition and another penitential element, such as the general confession, in the liturgy. A decision about this element of the liturgy needs to be made consultatively and before the liturgy begins.

During the Liturgy

The prayers need to be read in such a way that they can be clearly heard and understood by the liturgical assembly. This may call for some experimentation to find a suitable place in the church from which the prayers can be led. There is considerable value in always using the same place to read the prayers. If the building is large enough that most voices require amplification, the prayers may need to be read from the place where the lections are read. The practice of leading the intercessions from one's place in the congregation is often unhelpful and ought to be discouraged both because the intercessor's words are not always clearly audible to the assembly and because older people are often disconcerted by disembodied voices coming from unpredictable places. As people come more and more to adopt a standing posture for prayer, rather than kneeling with eyes closed, visibility and predictability of the location of the intercessor will be of more concern. Unlike during the gospel reading, the congregation will not be facing the person leading the prayers unless the leader is at the front of the congregation. This should be kept in mind as communities decide where the leader of the prayers should stand. Many people, particularly older people and the hearing impaired, find it difficult to listen to an "unseen" voice.

The intercessor, coming from his or her place within the congregation, moves to the designated place for the prayers when the presider stands to break the silence following the sermon. (If a creed is used, intercessors move to their place during the creed). Pausing briefly after arriving at their appointed place, intercessors may need to give *brief* instructions concerning posture or refrains. If a refrain is being used, it should be brief and easily memorable so that the congregation can respond easily at the end of each petition. At the conclusion of the prayers when all have responded with the final "Amen", the presider opens his or her arms to greet the people with the Peace. Once the people have begun to exchange the sign of peace, intercessors return to their place.

CHAPTER 5
CONFESSION AND ABSOLUTION

The celebration of the eucharist is itself the primary means by which the community of the baptized is reconciled both with one another and with God. The eucharist is the weekly renewal of our baptismal covenant with God. The basic prayer for forgiveness is the Lord's Prayer in which we pray, "Forgive us our sins as we forgive those who sin against us." All other verbal forms of confession and absolution must be seen, in the light of these, as modern additions to these basic elements.

Within the eucharist, reconciliation takes place in a variety of modes. The very act of sharing in the bread broken and the cup poured out is to share an action which is "for the forgiveness of sins" (Matt. 26:28). Reconciliation also takes place in the sharing of the peace. This is not only a human reconciliation but a reconciliation between individuals and God. For it is in the discovery of Christ in others that we are once again able to meet God. We learn from the First letter of John that one who says "I love God" and hates brother or sister is a liar; because if we cannot love the brother or sister whom we see, we cannot love God whom we are not able to see (I John 4:20).

The early church conceived of sin as something which affected the whole community. When one member of the Body was alienated from God by serious sin the whole Body was affected. By the time of the high middle ages this communal understanding of the nature of sin had diminished, and sin and its consequences came to be increasingly privatized with an emphasis on 'individual' sins. With the establishment of the church and later the dissolution of the empire during the barbarian invasions, the list of acts constituting serious sin increased to include anti-social acts and crimes against civil law. The relationship between sin and God's justice came to be equated with the nature of the relationship between crime and the civil courts.

Eucharistic liturgies did not begin to deal with formularies for confession until at least the eighth century. The formularies which do appear at this time appeared in the private devotions of the celebrant *before* mass. These devotions came to be extended to the laity in the late medieval period with the introduction of devotional books for lay use during the celebration of the eucharist. By this period the prevailing theology of the eucharist had changed from that of the corporate celebration of the Christian community, in which the saving acts of Christ are proclaimed, into the mystery of the descent of God onto the altar.

There had been a dramatic shift from community participation to humble adoration of 'the miracle of the Mass' effected by the priest. The first *Book of Common Prayer* simply borrowed these devotions from the *Lay-Folk's Mass-Book*, and Langforde's *Meditations in the Time of Mass* and thus uncritically retained and legitimized what had formerly been extra-liturgical piety. The Prayer Book reformers left the question of the origins and liturgical appropriateness of this penitential element unexamined and succeeding revisions of the *Book of Common Prayer* have done the same thing, with only occasional alterations of the wording of the text.

In the *BAS* the permissive rubrics require the presider to consider carefully the place of penitential material in the celebration of the eucharist, for no Eucharist is without some penitential element. Several options are provided: the breaking of bread, the Lord's Prayer and the acting out of the Peace may stand alone as the elements of penitence and reconciliation in the liturgy; the service may begin with the use of the penitential rite; a penitential petition may be used in the prayers of the people; or the confession and absolution may follow the prayers of the people. A decision should be made based on considerations of the liturgical day and season and the needs of the assembly. In no case are more than one of the last three options used in the same celebration.

The use of the penitential rite at the beginning of the service is particularly appropriate for the season of Lent. On Sundays after Epiphany or Pentecost a petition may be included in the prayers of the people. The confession and absolution which has been a normative part of our eucharistic liturgy for many years may be reserved for use on particular days or seasons such as Fridays (a traditional penitential day for the Church), Ember Days and during Advent.

In planning the liturgy the penitential formula must be placed in balance with the other elements of the liturgy. The communal and ecclesial dimension of the rite must be emphasized. The breaking of bread as the renewal of the baptismal covenant and the principal means of Christian reconciliation should remain primary. The Lord's Prayer, prayers of the people, and Peace ought to be given equal weight with any penitential formula. Finally, it is important that the flexibility that is inherent in the rite itself be maintained and reflected in the course of the liturgical year.

CHAPTER 6
THE PEACE

The Peace anticipates the reign of God. In the Peace we play at what it is to be a citizen of the peaceable kingdom which is yet to come. The Peace dramatizes our encounter with Christ in one another. In the Peace we act out the reconciliation which is to characterize the life of the Christian.

We are people who live in the 'meantime', between the resurrection and the fullness of the kingdom of God; the eucharist is a foretaste of the banquet which we will share together in that kingdom. Living in the 'meantime' means that making peace is sometimes difficult, but we become people whose lives are characterized by peace by repeatedly acting it out. We encounter Christ in a new way as we learn to love Christ in our brothers and sisters in the eucharistic assembly.

A helpful insight into this might be the practice of one Christian tradition. After the initial, verbal, exchange of the peace between presider and community, the members of this eastern tradition kiss one another using the exchange "Christ is revealed among us." "Blessed be the revelation of Christ!"

We cannot hate our sister or our brother and say that we love God (I John 4:20). In sharing the peace as a response to God's word we dramatize the biblical injunction wherein we are told that if we bring our gift to the altar and then remember that our sister or brother has something against us we must first go and make peace and then return and offer our gift (Matt. 5:23-24). The present position of the peace in the rite, between the liturgy of the word and the preparation of the gifts is the oldest place we know for the Peace (Justin Martyr's *First Apology*, 65 c. 155).

The business of living a life characterized by peace and reconciliation can be difficult. Acting that out liturgically can also be difficult. We need to recall that the baptismal font is the common womb of all Christians, for we, who are sisters and brothers, intimate expressions of embrace and kiss of peace are appropriate. It is also a reality that our cultural sensibilities sometimes make this expression difficult. Especially during the time when this element of the rite is being introduced the style of greeting needs to be appropriate to the needs and sensibilities of the members of the congregation.

At the same time the sharing of the Peace meets other pastoral needs whose existence may not have been anticipated. Many persons who live alone, widows, widowers, and others, find in the warm and personal exchange of the

Peace a brief respite from the loneliness and isolation which may characterize their lives. It has been the experience of those who attend the eucharist but do not speak the language of the place, that in the peace a common bond which does not need words is established. The lack of physical expression of affection in many North American families has affected our culture. Christians have an opportunity to be a leaven in society by re-experiencing this lost intimacy which is appropriate to brothers and sisters reborn and made one in the body of Christ.

Problems occasionally arise when congregations do not understand the dimensions of encounter, reconciliation and anticipation which are intended to be present in our expressions of Peace. It is important that the people do not perceive this time as a social event, a foretaste of the coffee hour. It is also inappropriate to seek out only one's friends while ignoring the stranger or the visitor. It is not a time to get acquainted or to share news; it is a recognition and acknowledgement of ourselves as linked in a common bond, united in Christ.

CHAPTER 7
THE PREPARATION OF THE GIFTS

As a response to God's goodness, Christians offer their gifts and their very lives to God. It is important to keep the collection and presentation of money and other gifts in kind in balance with the presentation and preparation of the bread and wine. It is appropriate that the bread, wine, money, and other gifts all be presented together in an offertory procession. Water, since it is not the work of human hands or the offering of our own labour has not traditionally been seen as a part of the offertory procession. Various members of the congregation should be asked to take part in this presentation, rather than reserving it for any specific group such as ushers, servers, or children. It is the life of the whole community that is represented in the act. This sense of communal offering is enhanced if, on occasion, the whole community presents gifts in an offertory procession. Harvest Thanksgiving is one particularly appropriate occasion when this could take place. The relationship between bread, wine, money and other gifts as symbols of our life and work is often obscured if the bread and wine are presented first and the money and other gifts only later, towards the end of a hymn. Communities might want to think of ways in which the unity of the action might be restored. In some parishes this might involve the choir singing an anthem while the collection is taken, all the gifts being presented after while a hymn is sung by the whole congregation. Other communities find that if they choose a long hymn (or a shorter hymn with interludes between verses) this provides enough time to gather the collection, present all the gifts together and to prepare them at the altar. Still other communities have found that placing a collection plate on the oblations table along with the bread and wine, with the food basket at the foot of the table, allows members of the community to place their gifts in both the plate and basket as they come into the church and then all the gifts may then be presented as the hymn at the preparation of the gifts begins.

If the bread and wine remain on a table at the back of the church or in the central aisle until they are presented, it would be appropriate for a collection plate or basket to be placed with them. This would help make clear that bread, wine, and money are all elements in the offering of the life of the Christian community. If a community regularly brings gifts for a food bank these offerings are appropriately included among the gifts presented in this procession, the basket for their collection sitting alongside the table bearing the bread, wine and collection plate or basket.

The rite makes no provision for an offertory sentence. These sentences were originally pieces of psalmody sung during the preparation of the gifts. They have since become mere vestiges and serve no purpose other than to indicate that the time for the preparation of the gifts has come. The shape of the liturgy itself indicates that after the Peace the preparation of the gifts is to begin. A Hymn, or appropriate choral or instrumental music may be used during the gathering of the gifts.

As the gifts are gathered, the assistants set the Lord's Table for the sacramental meal. It is particularly important at the preparation of the gifts that each assisting minister know their task and how it relates to the tasks of others. The mechanics of preparing the elements and vessels, of movement around the table and handling the vessels during the Great Thanksgiving, and of presiding over the distribution need to be practiced and gracious so that all seems to happen effortlessly. At the same time this needs to be done with the reverence due the mysteries of God.

Before the service, the chalice and paten, water, linens, and other necessary items are placed on a credence at the side of the chancel. There is no need for the chalice to be vested with a veil. While in many places it has been customary to place the vested chalice on the altar before the service, it is important to keep the altar bare until the preparation of the gifts when the focus of the service shifts to the altar.

The style in which the preparation of the gifts takes place will obviously vary from place to place. In some parishes where a forward altar is used and the liturgical style is less formal, it would be appropriate to have servers or assisting ministers place the fair linen and the candles on the altar at the time of the preparation of the gifts. This action is particularly helpful in emphasizing the Eucharist as a meal, an association which is often obscured by the traditional architecture and ceremonial which we have inherited. If this custom is adopted a corporal becomes unnecessary since it is itself the vestige of an altar cloth which has shrunk over time. If a corporal is used it is spread on the centre of the altar. The Deacon, if there is one, or assisting minister then brings the chalice and water to the altar. The purificator is placed to the right side of the corporal.

The rubrics direct that it is desireable that only one chalice and paten be on the altar during the Great Thanksgiving in order that the symbolism of one bread and one cup be preserved. If one chalice does not contain sufficient wine for the communion of the whole community additional wine may be placed on the altar in a clear glass pitcher or in a flagon. (Additional vessels needed to distribute communion are not brought to the altar until after the communion of the liturgical ministers.) The rubrics of the rite make it clear that care must be taken to place sufficient bread and wine on the altar during the preparation of the gifts so that any supplementary consecration is unnecessary. The chalice need not be covered with a pall except in situations where there is danger of foreign objects falling into the chalice or at times of year when there is danger of flies being attracted to the wine.

The sacramental signs of the Eucharist are eating and drinking. There should be an obvious association between the elements used in the Eucharist and elements associated with ordinary food and drink. Consequently, the type of bread used for the Eucharist is not a matter of indifference. A loaf that looks and tastes like bread enhances the realism of the sacramental sign of eating. Loaf bread may be used in either leavened or unleavened form. Appendix 3 (pp. 65-6) provides several recipes as well as other available resources. The nature of bread used for the Eucharist also has theologcial implications. The use of one loaf to be shared by all is fundamental to the concept of the Lord's Supper as set forth by Paul: "Because there is one bread, we who are many are one body, for we all partake of the one bread" (I Cor. 10:17). If the loaf is cut or broken before the liturgy (into cubes, for example,) this metaphor is seriously obscured. Loaf bread is best presented at the altar in a cloth-lined basket. The sense of community participation and offering is heightened if various members of the community take turns in baking bread for the Eucharist. If this is the custom, it would be appropriate to include the baker and members of their family among those who present the gifts in the offertory procession.

The use of wafers seriously distorts the image of unity found in a single loaf. It is also questionable whether the use of wafers evokes a sense of eating bread associated with a meal. This is particularly the case with young children who have great difficulty making the association between a wafer and anything they understand to be food. While some would argue that the advantage of wafers or hosts is that they are convenient to handle and easy to store, these advantages need to be weighed against the highly evocative images of the single loaf.

If a parish is to continue to use wafers it should consider the use of the heavier whole wheat type which tastes more like bread, and using only large wafers (rather than "peoples' hosts") from which a number of people can receive communion and which can be broken during the "breaking of bread". Wafers can be brought to the altar in a cloth-lined basket or a bread box. They are distributed either from that vessel, which is more convenient if there is a large number of communicants, or from a paten. Serious questions need to be posed about the continued use of ciboria. While these vessels were convenient when the use of "peoples' hosts" was widespread, they confuse the signs of eating and drinking when we continue to distribute bread from a vessel which is more clearly designed for drinking.

As parishes consider the signs of the sacramental meal and reconsider the type of bread they use, it would be appropriate to pose some questions about the type and quality of wine used in the eucharist. Is it appropriate to use wine of such low quality that members would never consider using it on their own table? As the wine becomes for us the Blood of Christ, we need to ask whether that symbol is impaired by the use of white, rather than red, wine.

The gifts of money, along with other gifts are received by assisting ministers who place them in a spot clearly visible to the congregation, preferably at the foot of the altar. (The tradition is that only those things that are specifically set aside or consecrated - bread, wine, oil - are placed on the altar itself during the Great Thanksgiving.) It is important that all the bread and wine to be consecrated for distribution be placed *upon* the altar during the preparation of the gifts. (The custom of having others stand about the table holding vessels of bread or wine which they will later distribute is a modern papal custom. Its introduction to Anglicanism seriously mars the sign of the whole assembly gathered to share in one holy food from the one table.)

After the gifts have been prepared (and any censing of them and the altar is completed) the presider's book or sacramentary is placed on the altar. Some reflection on the placement of the book would be appropriate. When the eucharist was celebrated in the eastward position, missal stands which held the book high above the altar and almost perpendicular to it appeared on many altars. As there were no sight lines to be blocked in this configuration, the matter was of little importance. This question needs to be reconsidered when celebrating the eucharist facing the people. It is important that the bread and the cup are the focus of attention on the altar. Devices such as missal stands and large cushions which draw attention to themselves diminish this centrality. The use of the missal stand and large cushions can easily be abandoned. The sacramentary can be placed directly on the altar either in front of the gifts or to their left or right, depending on where it can be most easily read by the presider. If some sort of support for the sacramentary is needed to avoid the reflection of strong overhead lighting, either small, unobtrusive, wooden stands or thin cushions can be purchased or made.

It is inappropriate if some gifts are given a greater dignity than others. There is no need, for example, to make signs of the cross over the money or to elevate the food basket. The gesture of presenting and receiving the gifts is sufficient.

The presider remains in the place from which he or she presided at the liturgy of the word while the gifts are prepared as this is normatively a liturgical ministry of others. In places where there is a deacon this is normatively a principal diaconal function, highlighting, as it does the servant character of this order, and reciprocally symbolizing to the community its own servant ministry. The minister preparing the gifts places the corporal in the centre of the altar in anticipation of the arrival of the gifts. Similarly the chalice is placed on the altar at this point. As the money and other gifts are received, the deacon or assistant prepares the bread and wine for the Great Thanksgiving. The loaf, in its basket, is placed on the corporal. Wine is poured from the flagon or cruet into the chalice, a small amount of water is customarily added. As the eucharistic prayer is the 'blessing' of the gifts of bread and wine it is inappropriate to anticipate this by making the sign of the cross over the water cruet. If more wine is needed the pitcher or flagon is set on the corporal behind the chalice. Chalice and paten could be set side by side so that they are both visible to the congregation (rather than perpendicular to the presider as has often been done). See Diagram 8.

Before proceeding with the rite, the presider may wash his or her hands. This action is a response to an age old human need to experience symbolic cleansing before we touch holy things. A deacon or a server carrying a bowl, or lavabo, in one hand, a towel on the same arm, and a pitcher of water in the other hand, goes to where the presider stands, pours water over the presider's hands, and, when the presider has dried his or her hands, returns the bowl and pitcher to the credence.

The presider now moves to the centre of the altar. The sign of the whole community gathered around the Lord's table may be enhanced by other ministers both ordained and lay standing behind the altar along with the presider. In many parishes where there is only one priest it is common to have two lay assistants stand on either side of the presider.

The so-called custom of concelebration is new to the modern western church. Its introduction into the Roman tradition at the time of the Second Vatican Council was an attempt to deal with that tradition's relatively recent sense of the obligation that fell on each priest to celebrate the daily eucharist. It is also related to the Roman system of Mass stipends. Neither of these concerns is relevant to our own Anglican tradition.

The liturgical result of these concerns often appeared more like simultaneous or synchronized celebration than the more primitive concelebration in which the college of presbyters stood round the altar as a sign of solidarity with their Bishop. Any division of the Eucharistic Prayer between a number of ministers standing at the altar detracts from the inherent unity of the prayer itself and the presidential character of the prayer which is prayed by the presider in the name of the whole community.

While it would be inappropriate for the other ministers at the altar to recite parts of the Eucharistic Prayer, and still more inappropriate to recite the entire prayer *sotto voce*, it would be entirely appropriate for other ministers at the altar to assume the *orans* position without implying that they are confecting the eucharist. In this sense this gesture is appropriate for all the people of God who gather to celebrate the Holy Eucharist (*BAS* p. 183).

All that has been offered on this occasion in both word and prayer as well as the actual gifts which are being presented, are offered to God as part of our "sacrifice of praise and thanksgiving". This is consistent with the Anglican theology which sees our offering not limited to bread and wine but including our "selves, our souls and bodies." This is made explicit in the Prayer over the Gifts which now follows the preparation of the table. The Prayer Book doxology "Blessed be thou Lord God of Israel for ever and ever; all that is in the heaven and earth are thine; all things come of thee of thine own have we given thee," anticipates the Great Thanksgiving and is not included in the *BAS* rite. Similarly, other formulae, particularly those ending with the response "Blessed be God forever", or the singing of the Doxology (Praise God from whom all blessings flow...) are inappropriate and ought not to be interpolated at this point.

CHAPTER 8
THE GREAT THANKSGIVING

The Great Thanksgiving is the heart of the eucharistic action. In it Christians offer, in praise and thanksgiving, their lives to God, both as community and individuals. It is the weekly proclamation of the saving works of God. Rooted in the table fellowship of Jesus, the eucharistic prayer takes the shape of the *Birkat ha Mazon*, the final prayer over the cup of the Jewish meal. Christians give thanks to God for the work of creation and redemption which culminates in the life and ministry of Jesus and is given a particular focus in the memorial of the Last Supper which Christians understand in the light of the resurrection meals in which the risen Lord "is known in the breaking of the bread."

The Presider, in praying the Great Thanksgiving, stands as the representative of the gathered community. It is important, then, that the attitude and gestures of the presider be as inclusive as possible, making it clear that the presider stands *in persona ecclesiae* and is not undertaking a work of private piety.

The Great Thanksgiving begins with the salutation and dialogue "Lift up your hearts" and concludes with the doxology and the great "Amen." Although in recent centuries only the preface and conclusion of the eucharistic prayer have been sung, it is evident that at one time the prayer was sung in its entirety just as were Jewish table prayers. In the period when priests began reciting the central portion of the prayer in secret, the music naturally dropped out. There is much to be said for giving consideration to the revival of the earlier practice, since the singing of the whole prayer emphasizes its special character and its unity (Presider's Edition, p.7). Presiders who have not been accustomed to singing the Eucharistic Prayer might wish to spend time with their church musician or some other person with musical skills to practice singing the text. Their are very few people who, with some patient effort, cannot learn to sing. As one music teacher has said, 'In 21 years of teaching, I never found a student without a voice. Sometimes it took a long time finding it.' When sung, the text should be proclaimed in the rhythm of clear and dignified speech, without undue haste on the one hand or delay on the other, and with a feel for the flow of the melodic line.

Proclaiming the eucharistic prayer is the privilege of the presider. It is not a prayer in which parts are delegated to others. If the presider cannot sing the dialogue and preface as noted in the Presider's Edition of the *BAS*, consideration might be given to singing the text to a simpler tone - even on a single tone. In no case should this part of the Great Thanksgiving be delegated to a cantor or assistant.

The Eucharistic Prayer is the great prayer of blessing sung over the bread and cup on the model of the Jewish table prayers of blessing. It is a prayer of faith addressed to God, an act of praise and thanksgiving for the whole work of creation and redemption. The prayer is a unity from the opening dialogue to the final doxology and Amen. As such, any change of physical position during the Eucharistic Prayer, for example, from standing to kneeling, obscures that unity and appears to give one portion of the prayer a greater dignity than another. In the Eucharistic Prayer the church expresses the meaning of the whole eucharistic action. Here the memorial anamnesis of redemption is made, and the church is united with Christ in offering and communion through the sanctifying power of the Holy Spirit.

On Gesture

When the eucharist is celebrated facing the people, presiders must become acutely aware of their gestures and manual actions during the Eucharistic Prayer. Actions that were perhaps meaningful to the presider when celebrating in the "eastward" position must be re-examined. Actions that are visible to the people need to be simple and self explanatory. Fussiness of gesture transforms the Great Thanksgiving from an act of prayer to one of clerical manipulation and obscures the character of the prayer. When celebrating facing the people simplicity and austerity of gesture assume a particular importance.

Often the gestures and manual acts of the presider have been a mystery to the congregation, a matter of "priestcraft", never having been explained to the congregation and, perhaps, never even having been appreciated entirely by the presider. It is said that the grandmother of the celebrated Anglican liturgist Dom Gregory Dix witnessed the Tridentine mass but once. After observing the actions of the priest during the Great Thanksgiving she remained convinced that the priest had released a crab on the altar and that it was his duty to keep the crab from crawling sideways into the view of the congregation. The story is extreme, but it does serve to remind presiders of how concealed or unexplained ritual gesture can be perceived. These minute manual gestures can be even more of a mystery to the people when the priest faces the congregation across the altar for the celebration.

With the revival of ritualism in the Anglican communion during the last century, more elaborate manual actions for the Eucharistic Prayer were adopted, usually without examination, from the Missal of Pius V. These actions, which were related to specific words and phrases in the Pian Missal, were transplanted in their entirety to the Prayer Book. Whereas rationales were provided for their use in terms of Catholic continuity and tradition, they sat ill with the Anglican text. They are even less suited to the words of the new Eucharistic Prayers. Thus gestures like the sign of the cross and multiple touchings of the elements are out of place in the new prayers. The eucharistic elements are consecrated through prayer and thanksgiving, not by manual acts. It is important not to create the impression that consecration is through manipulation of the elements.

In considering the appropriate gestures used during the eucharistic prayer, it is important that there be an intentional and reflected correlation between word and gesture. For example, during the salutation and *sursum corda* it is important that the gestures be those of inclusive greeting and invitation to lift our hearts to God rather than the purposeless tracing of circles in the air with no regard as to how these gestures fail to elaborate the words they accompany.

During the Eucharistic Prayer

The following manual actions are suggested. At the salutation, "The Lord be with you," the hands would be open and outstretched in the same manner as they were at the beginning of the liturgy for the apostolic greeting or for the Peace. See Diagram 3. The Presider's movements must be smooth and deliberate rather than abrupt and hasty. The size of the gesture should be appropriate to the size of the room and the proximity of the congregation. For example, gesture needs to be more exaggerated in a large Cathedral and more intimate when the whole community is gathered within a few feet of one another. At the words, "Lift up your hearts," the hands are raised from their extended position in an upward movement. (Diagram 5) At the words, "Let us give thanks to the Lord our God," the hands are returned to the initial gesture of greeting.

Beginning with the preface and throughout the Great Thanksgiving, the biblical gesture of praying with hands uplifted and outstretched, the *orans* position, which Christians have inherited from their Jewish forebears, is appropriate because it gives visual expression to the import of the words. For the Sanctus, the presider's hands are joined together. As the prayer continues after the Sanctus the presider raises hands to the *orans* position again and maintains this position up to the institution narrative. It is helpful if an assistant follows the eucharistic prayer in the Presider's Edition and turns pages when necessary. This allows the presider more freedom and a continuity of gesture. It can also help avoid the visual impression that the sacramentary is some kind of recipe book in which a formula is being followed. Should the presider need to turn pages he or she does not leave one hand extended while turning a page (or making a gesture) with the other hand. Both hands may be brought together before turning a page or making a gesture. A sense of visual balance can be maintained if, when turning a page, the hand not turning the page is simply placed on the table.

While a strict interpretation of the Canons of 1604 would perhaps lead the presider to join hands and bow at every mention of the name Jesus, when facing the people this appears needlessly busy and can be very distracting for the other

The Great Thanksgiving - Chapter 8

Diagram 5

Chapter 8 - *The Great Thanksgiving*

members of the eucharistic assembly. Bobbing the head at the name of Jesus is even more distracting as, unlike the more elaborate gesture, it is not obvious to the average observer what the presider intends and it appears very idiosyncratic. Here, again, the presider should reflect on the unity of the eucharistic prayer and avoid gestures which disrupt the integrity of the prayer.

A useful exercise would be for the presider to spend some time in front of a mirror practicing these gestures. It is important to have some sense of the relationship between the proportions of the presider's body and appropriate ritual gesture. Because our bodies come in various shapes and sizes, it is impossible to impose absolutely uniform postures on all presiders. At the same time presiders might notice the curious appearance of asymmetrical gestures.

It is important that presiders reflect carefully on the gestures they use during the Eucharistic Prayer. The theology of the Eucharistic Prayers as found in the *BAS* does not admit a position of 'moment of consecration'. Therefore it is important that ritual gesture not undermine this understanding of the whole Eucharistic Prayer as an act of praise and thanksgiving in which the bread and wine become for us the body and blood of Christ. The use of gesture, then, must not convey the impression that there is a particular 'moment' of change. From the perspective of those in the congregation, many have found it a freeing experience not having a moment of change identified by gesture. Thus, it is possible to maintain the *orans* position throughout the words concerning the bread and the cup.

At the same time, the presider may find it natural to associate words and gesture at this point. It is important, however, to remember that the institution narrative is a part of the eucharistic prayer which is offered to God with the whole community, and not an interpolated monologue when the priest speaks to the elements themselves. Throughout the words concerning the bread, the priest holds the bread in clear view of the people. (Diagram 6) Just as we do not drink from the cup at the words "Drink this", the bread is not broken during the institution narrative. This action occurs later. Because the eucharistic prayer has its roots in the Jewish table blessing, the bread is broken and distributed after the prayer of thanksgiving rather than in its midst. In the same way, throughout the words concerning the cup, the priest holds the cup before the people. (Diagram 7) Unlike the *BCP* there is no direction to touch the pitcher or flagon on the altar. The intention to consecrate has already been designated by placing the elements on the table during the preparation of the gifts. To insist on touching another vessel containing more wine transmits inappropriate messages about our understanding of eucharistic consecration.

Genuflections, elevations, bell-ringing or other acts of veneration at the time of the institution narrative are inconsistent with Anglican eucharistic theology, particularly with the theology of the new eucharistic prayers. Any implication that the dominical words alone consecrate, or that they can in any way be

Diagram 6

Chapter 8 - *The Great Thanksgiving*

Diagram 7

The Great Thanksgiving - Chapter 8

isolated from the eucharistic prayer as a whole, impairs the integrity of the *BAS* eucharistic prayers. Similarly, it is not appropriate to interpolate these acts of veneration after the *epiclesis*. In both these cases it is particularly important that there be some congruity between our eucharistic theology and ritual action.

As the prayer continues after the institution narrative the presider once again assumes the *orans* position praying with hands uplifted and outstretched. A number of the prayers contain a memorial acclamation ("Christ has died,..." or, "Dying you destroyed our death,...") sung or said by the entire congregation. The presider could appropriately join his or her hands during the singing of this acclamation. In Eucharistic Prayer 3, however, the whole community joins the presider in the *anamnesis* ("we remember his death,..."), a central element of eucharistic prayer. Since *anamnesis* is integral to eucharistic prayer itself, a change in gesture would be inappropriate.

For the *epiclesis* or prayer for the gift of the Holy Spirit, the presider may choose to adopt the ancient gesture associated with this prayer: hands together and outstretched over the bread and cup, palms down. (Diagram 8) After the *epiclesis* the presider returns hands to the *orans* position as the eucharistic prayer continues in asking for the fruits of communion.

The Doxology is the final ascription of praise and thanksgiving which calls for the assent of the congregation in the form of the "Great Amen". The presider raises the paten or basket containing the bread in one hand and the cup in the other, and sings or says the doxology. (Diagram 9) If there is a deacon assisting at the liturgy, it is normally their responsibility to elevate the chalice during the doxology. (Diagram 10) The elements continue to be held until after the community has responded, "Amen". This could be the appropriate place for the joyous ringing of bells.

After the presider (and deacon) has placed the vessels upon the altar, a profound bow or genuflection by all at the altar, as an act of reverence, would be appropriate. The presider and other ministers assume the *orans* position for the Lord's Prayer. As has been frequently mentioned this posture for prayer is the common possession of all Christians and is not reserved for the clergy or particular groups within the Church. During the recitation of the Lord's own prayer, it would be a particularly appropriate gesture to express the solidarity of all Christians in the Body of Christ for the whole congregation to join the presider in this posture of prayer.

While Anglicans have often felt uncomfortable with new gestures, many communities are discovering that their liturgical life is enriched and their sense of openness to God enhanced, when physical attitudes of prayer are added to the verbal. In this way, our worship becomes more fully an expression of our entire selves. Experience has shown that, because of their familiarity with the text and its central place in Christian prayer, communities incorporate a new posture

Diagram 8

The Great Thanksgiving - Chapter 8

Diagram 9

Chapter 8 - *The Great Thanksgiving*

Diagram 10

The Great Thanksgiving - Chapter 8

during the Lord's Prayer with more ease than at other points in the liturgy. Until the community becomes familiar with the gesture, the presider might introduce the prayer by saying, "As a sign of our openness to God, we raise our hands in prayer and sing/say:".

The Breaking of Bread

Since the earliest days of the Church, the "breaking of the bread" has been a technical name for the eucharist itself. It binds together elements which are both functional and symbolic. The bread is broken so that all may communicate. At the same time, in the action of the breaking of the bread, we cannot help but reflect on Jesus' feeding the multitudes, sharing with the poor, dining with friends, and revealing himself in the breaking of the bread at the supper at Emmaus and the other resurrection meals. The early Christian community also saw an eschatalogical dimension in the breaking of bread. Just as grain, once scattered on the hillsides, was gathered and made into the one bread, so too the Church will be gathered into God's reign through Christ (see *Didache* 9).

The *BAS* provides a variety of seasonal fraction sentences (or confractoria) that may be said or sung during the breaking of bread. The book also provides a number of anthems to be sung during the breaking of bread and communion (*BAS* pp. 226-228), including the familiar anthem "Lamb of God" which may be used instead of, or in addition to, the sentences. All of these anthems are intended to be sung rather than said.

During the confractorium it is important that the bread be clearly broken in the sight of the congregation. This action need not be rushed, particularly if one of the anthems is being sung. While it is not necessary at this point to break the bread into as many pieces as there are communicants, it is important that the symbolic character of "the one bread broken for the many, so that the many may become one" is clearly seen by the whole community.

The commixture (or dropping a part of the broken bread into the chalice) is a vestige of the ancient practices called the *fermentum*, when the consecrated bread was sent from the bishop's celebration to the parish churches, and the *sancta*, when consecrated bread reserved from a previous celebration was placed in the cup. (Both were intended as signs of the oneness of the eucharist in place and time). As both the *sancta* and the *fermentum* have disappeared from contemporary liturgical use, the vestige makes little sense and only tends to confuse the average observer. This custom should be allowed to join a number of ceremonies from the past which are no longer used.

At the invitation, which the rubrics make clear is to take place before any have communicated, the presider may hold up the bread in one hand and the cup in the other while looking at the people and saying, "The gifts of God for the people of God." As at the doxology the deacon may hold up the cup while the presider holds up the bread. See Diagram 10. This serves as a signal for the congregation to begin to move forward for communion.

CHAPTER 9
THE COMMUNION

After the congregation has begun to move forward for communion the presider and assistants receive communion as quickly and unostentatiously as they would expect members of the congregation to do. It is important to remember that communion is a gift both given and received. This could be made clear by several possible practices. The presider could communicate the assistant(s) first who would then give communion to the presider. Another practice might be to have an assistant communicate the presider who would, in turn, give communion to the assistants. In either case it is important to be seen to be given communion by someone else.

At this time additional vessels required for the communion — baskets or patens and chalices — are brought to the altar and filled with the consecrated bread and wine. When the number of communicants is large, several people should assist in the distribution. Even in a small congregation it is desirable that at least one other person assist in the distribution of communion.

Assisting ministers need not be ordained, in fact lay people are appointed for this ministry on principle. The presider is assisted by others whose ministries contribute to the whole work of worship so that the diversity of liturgical ministers will reflect the wholeness of the people of God.

A communion procession, in which the whole congregation moves forward to receive the sacrament of the body and blood of Christ, is one of the more ancient elements in the public celebration of the liturgy. In order to emphasize the corporate dimension of the procession and the act of communion itself, the procession might be accompanied by a communion psalm. Lead by the choir or cantor, a hymn or a psalm of thanksgiving, with a simple and memorable antiphon for the people, sung as they move up to receive communion, evokes the sense of unity that is inherent in corporate song. The whole community gives thanks that they are being fed and nourished on Christ's body and blood so that they will be sustained for the work of the body of Christ in the world.

The use of communion stations on the floor of the nave is an efficient way of distributing the sacrament, and makes the receiving of communion much easier for the infirm. The presider who distributes the bread might remain in the centre aisle and the assisting ministers, each with a chalice, might stand on either side. Keeping some space between the minister with the bread and the minister(s) with the chalice gives communicants time to chew the bread before receiving the wine. The signs of eating and drinking are primary to the sacramental meal and should be heightened rather than diminished. When the congregation is large, pairs of ministers may be stationed at various points in the aisle so that communion may be distributed without undue delay. When planning the location of communion stations it is important to reflect on their relationship to the altar. It is in the context of a meal that we recognize the Lord "in the breaking of the bread." It is important, then, not to loose the relationship between table and communion by placing great distances between station and altar.

It is important to achieve a balance between the personal and public aspect of receiving holy communion. The moment of reception is an intensely personal appropriation of what is being celebrated corporately. The pace of distribution must be such that the minister can address the words of distribution to each communicant. It is important, however, that these words not be so rushed that the communicant is not able to respond "Amen" before receiving communion. In the *BAS* the words of distribution are designed so as to make this possible in every case.

In many parishes 'sidesmen' or ushers have had the responsibility of indicating to communicants when it is time to leave their pews. While the intention of this has been to assure a sense of seemliness and order, it often appears as if their responsibility is to hold people back rather than urge them forward. In parishes where communion processions are the practice, it is important that there is a sense of the whole assembly moving together towards the altar. Experience has shown that this movement is self-regulating and can be impaired by ushers letting people move only a pew at a time. In parishes where people receive at the altar rail, ushers help best by not holding people back but by encouraging them to move forward, ensuring that there are no gaps at the rail.

For communion, care needs to be taken with the way in which the bread and cup are received, particularly if a communion procession is used. When whole bread is used, the people should be instructed to place one hand on top of the other to receive the bread. This instruction is particularly important to avoid the problem of crumbs falling between cupped hands or the bread crumbling if received between the thumb and forefingers. The ministers deliver the bread without any ceremony which detracts from the act of giving (such as signs of the cross, squeezing of hands or the breaking of wafers). The receiving of the sacrament itself is the primary sign from which nothing should be allowed to detract.

In receiving the chalice communicants should take a firm hold on it and guide it to their lips. This is particularly important in a communion procession, because in a standing position it is difficult for the minister with the cup to have a sense of when the communicant has actually drunk from the cup. If communicants take the chalice into their own hands, care must be taken to assure that there is always a firm hand on the cup.

The question of how to administer communion to young children and infants is being asked with increasing frequency. Young children can be given bread in the same way as an adult, but some do not like the taste of wine and should not be forced to receive from the cup. Infants can be given a very small particle of bread, or simply a few drops of wine on the tip of a finger placed in their mouth. It is important in distributing communion to children that in the words of administration the bread and wine are associated with the body and blood of Christ rather than statements like, "Jesus loves you". Children are open to ritual activity and language. Hearing the words of distribution instills within children a naturalness about Christ's presence in the eucharistic mystery. Later, as children grow older, they may ask questions about the nature of Christ's presence, but will not be repelled by the idea, as teenagers so often were in the days when first communion followed confirmation.

After communion has been shared by the community, it is appropriate that the various deacons and lay members of the community who are delegated to take communion to the sick and shut in approach the altar where they may collect the pyx or communion kit needed for their ministry. It is important that this be seen as a public act and that the communion of those impaired from being present at the parish eucharist by age or sickness are not separated from communion with the local church. In some communities the sense of solidarity with separated members of the parish has being heightened if the presider makes a simple statement like: "Take the sacrament which we have shared to N & N who are one with us in the Body of Christ." Those taking the sacrament to the sick or shut-in would leave the church quietly while those appointed to clear the altar would proceed with their duties.

After all have received communion a space for prayerful thanksgiving and reflection is appropriate. This may take the form of a space of corporate silence. It could also take the form of a communion hymn (in which the congregation gives thanks for the gifts received and asks for the grace to act out what is being accomplished within them), a piece of music written to encourage corporate meditation (such as some of Jaques Berthier's music written for the community of Taizé), or the continued singing of the psalm and antiphon used during the communion procession itself.

The rubrics in the *BAS* allow for the ablutions to be done either after the people have been dismissed or immediately after the communion. Both in the early church and throughout most of Anglican history the ablutions were normally performed in the sacristy after the people had left. We would do well to restore this practice. An extended cleansing of the vessels in full view of the congregation can easily overshadow other elements of the liturgy which are of considerably greater importance. Even common table custom would dictate that dishes are done after the meal, and in the kitchen, rather than the dining room!

If the ablutions are to be performed during the liturgy it is best that they not take place at the altar but in the sacristy or at a side table or credence as quickly and unobtrusively as possible. The bread is consumed and crumbs are emptied into the chalice. The wine is consumed and the chalice is rinsed. Water is sufficient for this rinsing. There is no reason why the ablutions may not be done by someone other than the presider, including lay persons.

CHAPTER 10
THE CONCLUDING RITE

Just as the shape and purpose of the gathering of the community has become obscured over time by a series of diverse elements from different sources, so too the concluding rites have experienced the same liturgical phenomenon. As parishes use the *BAS* eucharistic rite, it is particularly important that they reflect on the shape and purpose of the concluding rite and re-examine their current practice.

The intention of this part of the service is to give thanks for Christ's self-giving in the eucharist, to ask that we may bear the fruit of that gift in our lives, and to be sent out into God's world in Christian mission. To do this, we need to be careful about how we use the concluding rites so as not to obscure their purpose. This may involve a fairly radical restructuring of what has become local custom.

After the distribution of communion (and the ablutions, if they are done during the liturgy) the presider and assistants return to where they presided at the ministry of the word. When the communion music is over, or after a space of silence, the presider and assistants stand and the presider bids the people to stand and pray with the words, "Let us pray."

Prayer After Communion

The Prayer after Communion may take one of three possible forms. The first is the use of the variable Prayer after Communion, which is found with the Proper of the Day in the Presider's Edition. In some communities this prayer, followed by the people's "Amen" and dismissal, may be all that is needed to conclude the rite. Other communities may wish a more fulsome response for the people, in which case the doxological response would be added. The presider says, "Glory to God," and all then continue, "whose power working in us can do infinitely more than we can ask or imagine...." Some communities have found it helpful to omit the doxology during Lent and to return to its use at Easter. The variable Prayer after Communion is thematically related to the other prayers in each set of propers and asks that we be given grace to bear a variety of fruits in the Christian life, the emphasis of which appropriately varies from week to week throughout the cycle of the Christian year.

The third form of the Prayer after Communion is the fixed one printed in the *BAS*. It begins with the versicle and response, "All your works praise you, O

Lord. And your faithful servants bless you." Together the community continues with the prayer: "Gracious God, we thank you for feeding us...." The decision as to which form will be used is made when planning the liturgy and not at the last moment. The rubrics are clear that the variable form and the fixed form are not both to be used at the same celebration.

The Dismissal

Following the Prayer after Communion the community is sent out by the deacon or an assistant with the appointed words of dismissal. It is important that these words be said from the front of the church rather than after the clergy and choir have processed to the back so as to avoid any appearance of clericalization, and to emphasize that it is all God's people who, nourished by eucharistic gifts, go out to enact the ministries that are theirs by right of their baptism.

Just as the procession at the entrance varies with the shape and size of the building and the liturgical day, so too does the final procession. In small buildings where the liturgy simply begins when all are in their places and the presider greets the congregation, there is no need for any sort of formal procession at the end of the service. Larger congregations might wish to vary the style of final procession according to the day of the liturgical year. While on Principle Feasts it could be appropriate to have a procession down the centre aisle to the back of the church, on most Sundays a simple procession, in which the ministers leave the chancel by a shorter route, could be suitable. Where feasible, it could be an important sign of the ministry of the whole body to encourage members of the congregation to join the liturgical ministers in the procession out of the church. A decision of this nature must be made with care and attention to the nature of the local liturgical space and the sensibilities of the community.

The service comes to a prompt and unembellished conclusion. Nothing is added that would diminish the sense that the whole community, ordained and lay, fulfills its worship of God by together going out in mission. Accordingly it is inappropriate to encourage the laity to kneel in prayer after the procession has passed.

If a hymn is to form a part of the concluding rite, its appropriate place is after the distribution of communion and before the Prayer after Communion. In choosing these hymns, those of praise and thanksgiving as well as those which help make the transition from the worship of the gathered community to the service of Christ in the world are particularly appropriate. The rubrics of the eucharist do not anticipate a hymn being sung as the liturgical ministers leave after the dismissal.

The *BAS* does have a number of rubrics indicating where hymns may appropriately be sung, there is no such rubric after the dismissal. While this will be a departure from the custom of many parishes the change in the *BAS* is intentional. The purpose of the dismissal is to bring the liturgy to a close and to send the whole community out into the world. Singing a hymn at this point draws people back into liturgical activity which has been brought to an end. By not singing a hymn we avoid obscuring the shape and purpose of the concluding rite and reserve song for those times when the procession at the end of the liturgy is leading the congregation out to further liturgical activity (as in the rubric of the funeral liturgy on p. 586).

Blessings

The question of blessings before the dismissal needs to be re-thought. The practice of episcopal blessings at the end of the liturgy has been a part of the tradition probably since the late patristic period. These blessings were, however, restricted to bishops and were not given by presbyters. Presbyteral blessings began to take on a widespread character only in the 12th century by which time the laity normally only received communion once a year, even though they assisted at the eucharist at least each Sunday. In this context, the blessing took the place of the actual reception of communion. With the restoration of eucharistic practice, in which communicants normally receive the sacrament at each celebration of the eucharist, there is no longer a pastoral need for a blessing as a substitute for communion. It ought to be a particular theological concern that we do nothing after the reception of communion that would in any way foster a sense that Christ's self giving in the eucharist needs to be supplemented. Sometimes it would appear that the blessing is given greater liturgical importance than the act of communion itself. Accordingly, congregations which do not have large numbers of non-communicants present need not have a blessing as part of the concluding rite.

Postludes

The use of a postlude which encourages the congregation to sit, rather than leave, seriously impairs the intention of the concluding rite. Many congregations are discovering that there is no need for any sort of music to accompany their departure from the liturgical space. Musicians are also coming to appreciate not having to play at a time when their performance often goes unheard or simply serves as background music. While in Cathedrals and other churches of similar size, a postlude may be desireable to accompany the procession of a large choir and numerous liturgical ministers, in most Canadian parishes the postlude is unnecessary. If a community chooses to have all its members join in the procession, then it might be appropriate to accompany this action with suitable music, giving the sense that this is the final part of the liturgical activity. The custom of applauding after a postlude is regrettable, exalting, as it does, one particular ministry above others and forms a sense of performance rather than liturgical offering.

APPENDIX 1
LITURGICAL COLOUR

When colour began to be used intentionally in liturgical vesture, it was of two types, light and dark. The first was used for festivals and times of celebration, the other for times of preparation, penance, and grief. It is basically this system of light and dark colours which continues to be used in the Byzantine and Eastern Churches. In time, particularly in the West, the range of colours became more carefully regulated, although various parts of the church maintained their own sequence of colours. Some places made do with only one or two colours, others used many more than are now common.

The revival of liturgical colour by Anglicans in the last century saw the introduction of the Roman five colour sequence in most places. While a sequence of colours does have a teaching dimension, the particular sequence used is not one of absolute law. Parishes may feel free to refine sequences of colour that express their own particular community life and the resources they have available. In some places this may mean a return to fewer colours; in others an increased number. In doing this, however, parishes need to recognize that they are a part of a universal Church in which the use of colour is not idiosyncratic but follows particular patterns.

This increased flexibility has enabled parishes to do a number of things. For example, parishes can be more relaxed about the variety of colours incorporated in festive vestments. Particularly when artists are commissioned to create festive vestments the use of yellows, oranges and golds as well as the traditional white can enhance the joyful character of the celebration. This flexibility also makes possible a distinction between the liturgical character of Advent and Lent. Advent is a season of preparation that does not have the penitential aspects of Lent. Since it has often been the custom to embroider symbols of the passion (crowns of thorns, nails, etc.) on purple vestments, the piety associated with Lent has been transferred to the season of Advent because the vestments were worn during both seasons giving people the impression that Advent was a "little Lent." As the readings and proper prayers make a very clear distinction in the character of the two seasons, returning to the tradition in which deep blue was the Advent colour, and either violet or unbleached linen was the Lenten colour this confusion of seasons can be avoided and the distinctive character of each highlighted.

Appendices

APPENDIX 2
INCENSE

The use of incense has been part of the ceremonial of the church for most of its history, both before and after the Reformation. While its use in primitive worship may have been originally to disinfect, it was clearly associated in the Hebrew Scriptures with cleansing and prayer ('Let my prayer be set forth in your sight as incense...' Ps. 141). Over the last few years the use of incense has increased widely within Canadian Anglicanism and has become a part of the worshipping life of a wide variety of parishes, many of whom would not have dreamed of using it even a decade ago. This is perhaps a reflection on an increased awareness that all the senses are appropriately involved in the worship of God and a growing openness to the variety of ways in which ritual activity can enrich our experience of corporate worship.

If incense is new in a parish as well as if incense has had a part in the worship of a parish for a long time, its use in conjunction with the BAS needs careful consideration. Where incense has been used in the liturgies of the Prayer Book, the ceremonial has usually been adapted directly from the Roman Rite. A much simpler use of incense would be appropriate with the new rites, involving a less elaborate censing of things and persons and, perhaps, a re-consideration of frequency of use in the context of the liturgy. A careful reflection on how and when incense is used is particularly important when its use is new to a community.

In the eucharist, the primary use of incense centres on the preparation of the gifts and the eucharistic prayer. Other occasions, in descending order of importance, are the Gospel procession and at the Gathering of the Community.

While the gifts are being presented and prepared, a thurifer brings the thurible to the presider (who is still at the place from which the liturgy of the word is presided), who places incense on the coals. When the gifts have been prepared, the presider goes to the altar and is given the thurible by the thurifer. The presider then censes the gifts. While the traditional manner of censing the gifts may still be used, it might be important in places where incense is new to use a much less elaborate form for censing the gifts. This might consist of simply making a number of swings of the thurible in the direction of the gifts.

The presider then censes the altar, moving around the altar in a counter-clockwise direction. If there is a cross behind the altar, it may be censed while the presider pauses in front of the altar. When the presider and assistant have returned to their original place behind the altar, the thurible is returned to the thurifer, who may then remain at the side of the altar, or some distance behind the presider, gently swinging the thurible throughout the eucharistic prayer and Lord's Prayer when the thurible is returned to the sacristy.

Alternatively, after the censing of the gifts and altar, the presider, the deacon or the thurifer may proceed to cense the sanctuary and the congregation. This censing, in particular, needs simplification. The hierarchical censing of individuals is to be discouraged.

The use of incense to cense persons or objects has traditionally been seen as a way of honouring the person or object being censed. It is important, therefore, that the censing of the congregation be seen as an honouring of the baptismal dignity of all present and not simply as a milling about among the congregation for fumigatory purposes or the establishment of a liturgical hierarchy in the liturgical assembly.

This censing may be accomplished in a variety of ways. The person doing the censing may move throughout the congregation and sanctuary, gently swinging the thurible as they walk, remembering that the purpose of this is to cense the people and the swinging action should, therefore, make this evident. (If this form of censing is adopted the hymn or organ voluntary must be long enough to cover the action). Alternatively, the person doing the censing may go to the chancel step and cense the congregation. A single swing of the thurible "full chain" toward the centre, right and left is sufficient. The thurifer may then face the sanctuary and cense all those in it in similar fashion. In some settings it may be more convenient to cense the sanctuary and then the congregation.

If incense is used during the proclamation of the Gospel, the following pattern is suggested. After the second reading, the thurifer brings the thurible and incense to the presider who puts incense on the coals. The thurifer then leads the procession towards the centre of the church and stands to one side as the others take their places. When the Gospel has been announced, the thurible is handed to the reader who censes the Gospel book (not the airspace on either side) and then hands the thurible back to the thurifer. The thurifer may then swing the thurible gently at "full chain" while the Gospel is read, taking care not to detract attention from the reading.

If incense is used during the entrance, it is carried before the cross and candles. Incense is put on the coals before the procession begins. In procession the thurible is swung gently and should not become the primary focus of attention. The altar may be censed after the apostolic greeting, during the opening song of praise (hymn, canticle, psalm, Glory to God, Kyrie, or Trisagion). On festivals when a hymn is sung in procession, the censing may take place once the presider has arrived in the sanctuary as the hymn continues to be sung.

At the end of the liturgy, unless the whole community is moving to further liturgical activity (eg. leading the procession at a funeral) the thurible would not normally be used in the final procession.

Appendices

APPENDIX 3
BREAD RECIPES

"Altar Bread"

This recipe can be made in bulk and the loaves frozen for use over a number of weeks, or made in a smaller batch for use on one or two Sundays.

Pre-heat oven to 350°F

    5 lb. whole wheat flour   1 2/3 c. honey
    4 egg yolks   4 1/2 c. lukewarm water
    1 2/3 c. olive oil   a pinch of salt

Add the egg yolks and oil to the flour and salt and blend thoroughly (works best with fingers); then add the honey and blend thoroughly. Add the lukewarm water in small doses, continually kneading to make sure the texture remains even throughout. (Exact amount of water should be determined by wetness of dough, don't let it get too sticky. If it does, add a little extra flour.)

Flatten the dough into patties 4 - 6 inches in diameter and about 5/8 - 3/4 inches thick. The loaves may be scored with a knife or cookie cutter before baking so that they can be more easily broken. Bake on an ungreased cookie sheet at 350 degrees until golden brown. Baking time is about 10-12 minutes per side, the method which seems to produce the best result is 12 min. on the first side and then 9-10 min. on the second. Some experimentation may be necessary. This mixture will yield 3 dozen loaves, about 4 inches in diameter.

The loaves can also be made 6 inches in diameter in order to communicate more people from the same loaf. The smaller loaves communicate approximately 25-30 people. The larger loaves communicate approximately 45-50 people.

Smaller batch quantities.

    3 c. whole wheat flour   1/3 cup honey
    1 egg yolk   3/4 - 1 c. lukewarm water
    1/3 c. olive oil   pinch of salt.

Follow directions as above.

"Syrian Bread"

5 lb. all-purpose flour
2 pkgs. dry activated yeast
3 tsp. salt
lukewarm water

Mix dry ingredients thoroughly and then add enough lukewarm water to make the mixture doughy. Let rise 15 min., then knead. Let rise 2-3 hours. Separate into balls 3-3 1/2 inches in diameter and allow to rise until doubled. Flatten balls until 1/2 to 3/4 inch thick. Cook the bottom of the bread on a griddle for about 1 min. or until brown and the top under the broiler for the same length of time. Makes about 15 loaves.

"Eucharistic Bread"

1 1/2 c. whole wheat flour
3/4 c. white flour
3/4 tsp. baking soda
2 T. shortening at room temp.
3/4 tsp. baking soda
3/4 c. cold water
3 T. honey

Mix the flour, soda, and salt thoroughly. Add the shortening. Blend by hand very well. Add the water and honey. Knead the dough until a light fluffy texture. Divide the dough into four loaves (three small and one larger). Bake for 20 to 25 min. until the loaves are firm to the touch.

A good resource book for other bread recipes is:
<u>Living Bread: Recipes for Home-baked Breads for the Eucharist and for the Fellowship and Family Tables.</u>; by Christine Whitehorn Stugard, Forward Movement Publications 1983.

APPENDIX 4
RESOURCES FOR SINGING THE GRADUAL PSALMS

Among the many available resources for singing the psalms there are several composed specifically for *The Book of Alternative Services:*

i. *Music for the Sunday Psalms* and *Music for Psalms for Holy Days*, George Black (Anglican Book Centre Toronto). These psalms are available for Years A, B and C, and are published in quarterly packets.

ii. *The PSALMS for use with The Book of Alternative Services of the Anglican Church of Canada*, John Galienne (Mrs. John Galienne, P.O. Box 475, Kingston, Ontario, K7L 4W5)

In the following resources, the calendar and lectionary used are either those of the present American Prayer Book or the Roman Lectionary both of which differ in some places from the Common Lectionary as found in The *Book of Alternative Services.* If you plan on using them, you should check to make sure the psalms are the same as those appointed in the Canadian lections.

i. *Gradual Psalms*, (The Church Hymnal Corporation, New York, 1981-1986). *BAS* translation. This is a series of volumes for Sundays of Lectionary years A, B and C as well as for Principal Feasts, Holy Days, Memorials and Commemorations.

ii. *The Grail Gelineau Psalter*, (G.I.A. Publications Inc., Chicago, 1972). Grail translation. This translation also appears in *The Gelineau Gradual* which has the gradual psalms from the *temporale* and other rites in the *Ordo Lectionum Missae.*

If you intend to use the Grail Psalter you would do well to acquire a copy of *The Psalms: An Inclusive Language Version Based on the Grail Translation from the Hebrew*, (G.I.A.Publications Inc., Chicago, 1986) and make the necessary adjustments in language to the musical edition of the gradual.

iii. *The Psalmnary: Gradual Psalms for Cantor and Congregation*, James E. Barrett. (The Hymnary Press, 1317 Sorenson Road, Helena MT 59601, 1982). *BAS* translation.

iv. *The Ionian Psalter*, (Ionian Arts Inc., P.O. Box 259, Mercer Island, Washington 98040-02590) Complete Gradual Psalms for American *BCP* and *Lutheran Book of Worship* lectionaries. Parts for congregation, SATB choir, and organ. Perhaps the most challenging musically of the resources available.

Appendices